FORCED MIGRATION & MORTALITY

Roundtable on the Demography of Forced Migration
Committee on Population
Holly E. Reed and Charles B. Keely, Editors

Commission on Behavioral and Social Sciences
and Education
National Research Council

National Academy Press
Washington, D.C.

NATIONAL ACADEMY PRESS 2101 Constitution Avenue, N.W. Washington, D.C. 20418

NOTICE: The project that is the subject of this report was approved by the Governing Board of the National Research Council, whose members are drawn from the councils of the National Academy of Sciences, the National Academy of Engineering, and the Institute of Medicine. The members of the committee responsible for the report were chosen for their special competences and with regard for appropriate balance.

This study was supported by a grant to the National Academy of Sciences by the Andrew W. Mellon Foundation. Any opinions, findings, conclusions, or recommendations expressed in this publication are those of the authors and do not necessarily reflect the views of the organizations or agencies that provided support for the project.

Suggested citation: National Research Council (2001) *Forced Migration and Mortality*. Roundtable on the Demography of Forced Migration. Committee on Population. Holly E. Reed and Charles B. Keely, eds. Commission on Behavioral and Social Sciences and Education. Washington, D.C.: National Academy Press.

Library of Congress Cataloging-in-Publication Data

Forced migration and mortality / Roundtable on the Demography of Forced
Migration, Committee on Population ; Holly E. Reed and Charles B. Keely,
editors ; Commission on Behavioral and Social Sciences and Education,
National Research Council.
   p. cm.
Chiefly papers presented at a workshop organized by the Roundtable on
the Demography of Forced Migration, held in Nov. 1999 in Washington,
D.C.
Includes bibliographical references and index.
  ISBN 0-309-07334-0 (pbk.)
  1. Refugees—Mortality—Congresses. 2. Forced migration—Congresses.
I. Reed, Holly. II. Keely, Charles B. III. Roundtable on the Demography
of Forced Migration. IV. National Research Council (U.S.). Committee on
Population. V. National Research Council (U.S.). Commission on
Behavioral and Social Sciences and Education
  HV640 .F57 2001
  304.6'4—dc21
2001000942

Additional copies of this report are available from National Academy Press, 2101 Constitution Avenue, N.W., Lockbox 285, Washington, D.C. 20055; (800) 624-6242 or (202) 334-3313 (in the Washington metropolitan area); Internet, http://www.nap.edu

THE NATIONAL ACADEMIES
National Academy of Sciences
National Academy of Engineering
Institute of Medicine
National Research Council

The **National Academy of Sciences** is a private, nonprofit, self-perpetuating society of distinguished scholars engaged in scientific and engineering research, dedicated to the furtherance of science and technology and to their use for the general welfare. Upon the authority of the charter granted to it by the Congress in 1863, the Academy has a mandate that requires it to advise the federal government on scientific and technical matters. Dr. Bruce M. Alberts is president of the National Academy of Sciences.

The **National Academy of Engineering** was established in 1964, under the charter of the National Academy of Sciences, as a parallel organization of outstanding engineers. It is autonomous in its administration and in the selection of its members, sharing with the National Academy of Sciences the responsibility for advising the federal government. The National Academy of Engineering also sponsors engineering programs aimed at meeting national needs, encourages education and research, and recognizes the superior achievements of engineers. Dr. William A. Wulf is president of the National Academy of Engineering.

The **Institute of Medicine** was established in 1970 by the National Academy of Sciences to secure the services of eminent members of appropriate professions in the examination of policy matters pertaining to the health of the public. The Institute acts under the responsibility given to the National Academy of Sciences by its congressional charter to be an adviser to the federal government and, upon its own initiative, to identify issues of medical care, research, and education. Dr. Kenneth I. Shine is president of the Institute of Medicine.

The **National Research Council** was organized by the National Academy of Sciences in 1916 to associate the broad community of science and technology with the Academy's purposes of furthering knowledge and advising the federal government. Functioning in accordance with general policies determined by the Academy, the Council has become the principal operating agency of both the National Academy of Sciences and the National Academy of Engineering in providing services to the government, the public, and the scientific and engineering communities. The Council is administered jointly by both Academies and the Institute of Medicine. Dr. Bruce M. Alberts and Dr. William A. Wulf are chairman and vice chairman, respectively, of the National Research Council.

ROUNDTABLE ON THE DEMOGRAPHY
OF FORCED MIGRATION

CHARLES B. KEELY (*Chair*), Walsh School of Foreign Service, Georgetown University

RICHARD BLACK, School of African and Asian Studies, University of Sussex

BRENT BURKHOLDER,* South East Asia Regional Office, World Health Organization, and International Emergency and Refugee Health Program, Centers for Disease Control and Prevention, Atlanta, Georgia

GILBERT BURNHAM, Center for Refugee and Disaster Studies, School of Public Health, Johns Hopkins University

WILLIAM GARVELINK, U.S. Agency for International Development, Eritrea

STEVEN HANSCH, Center for Disaster and Humanitarian Assistance Medicine, Uniformed Services University of the Health Sciences, Bethesda, Maryland

KENNETH HILL, Center for Refugee and Disaster Studies, School of Public Health, Johns Hopkins University

BELA HOVY, Division of Operational Support, United Nations High Commissioner for Refugees, Geneva

ALLAN JURY, Bureau of Population, Refugees, and Migration, U.S. Department of State

JENNIFER LEANING, François-Xavier Bagnoud Center for Health and Human Rights, School of Public Health, Harvard University

STEPHEN LUBKEMANN, Watson Institute for International Studies, Brown University

CAROLYN MAKINSON, The Andrew W. Mellon Foundation, New York

SUSAN FORBES MARTIN, Institute for the Study of International Migration, Georgetown University

ERIC NOJI, National Center for Infectious Diseases, Centers for Disease Control and Prevention, Atlanta, Georgia

W. COURTLAND ROBINSON, Center for Refugee and Disaster Studies, School of Public Health, Johns Hopkins University

SHARON STANTON RUSSELL, Center for International Studies, Massachusetts Institute for Technology

PAUL SPIEGEL,** International Emergency and Refugee Health Program, Centers for Disease Control and Prevention, Atlanta, Georgia

BARRY STEIN, Department of Political Science, Michigan State University

DAVID TURTON, Refugee Studies Centre, University of Oxford

RONALD WALDMAN, Mailman School of Public Health, Columbia University

ANTHONY ZWI, Department of Public Health and Policy, London School of Hygiene and Tropical Medicine

---

*Through December 1999.
**As of January 2000.

vii

CONTRIBUTORS

BRENT BURKHOLDER, South-East Asia Regional Office, World Health Organization, and International Emergency and Refugee Health Program, Centers for Disease Control and Prevention, Atlanta, Georgia

GILBERT BURNHAM, Center for Refugee and Disaster Studies, School of Public Health, Johns Hopkins University

MANUEL CARBALLO, International Centre for Migration and Health, Geneva, and Mailman School of Public Health, Columbia University

STEVEN HANSCH, Center for Disaster and Humanitarian Assistance Medicine, Uniformed Services University of the Health Sciences, Bethesda, Maryland

PATRICK HEUVELINE, Population Research Center, National Opinion Research Center, and University of Chicago

KENNETH HILL, Center for Refugee and Disaster Studies, School of Public Health, Johns Hopkins University

CHARLES B. KEELY, Walsh School of Foreign Service, Georgetown University

MYUNG KEN LEE, School of Public Health, Johns Hopkins University

DOMINIQUE LEGROS, Epicentre/Médecins Sans Frontières, Paris

PIERRE NABETH, Epicentre/Médecins Sans Frontières, Paris

CHRISTOPHE PAQUET, Institut de Veille Sanitaire, Paris

HOLLY E. REED, Committee on Population, Division on Behavioral and Social Sciences and Education, National Research Council

W. COURTLAND ROBINSON, Center for Refugee and Disaster Studies, School of Public Health, Johns Hopkins University

PETER SALAMA, International Emergency and Refugee Health Program, Centers for Disease Control and Prevention, Atlanta, Georgia

PAUL SPIEGEL, International Emergency and Refugee Health Program, Centers for Disease Control and Prevention, Atlanta, Georgia

RONALD J. WALDMAN, Mailman School of Public Health, Columbia University

Preface

Over the last few years, there has been a growing appreciation of the need for more information about complex humanitarian emergencies in order to develop understanding about and more effective reactions to such events. The number, frequency, magnitude, and sheer difficulty of forced migrations in recent history have contributed to the need for more data. In addition, operational personnel realize that cumulative knowledge does not simply emerge from repetitions of prior experience. Insight, better protocols, and more effective reactions require analysis, comparison, and testing new approaches. To accomplish this, the field needs systematic data collection to assess behaviors, to ask questions, and to formulate alternatives.

Demographers and epidemiologists can provide some of these services. These population-related disciplines have long histories of applied work, based on the mathematical and statistical methods they have developed. They have not built up a cumulative body of knowledge, however, about complex emergencies.

In response to the need for more information about the measurement and estimation of displaced populations and their vital rates, the Committee on Population held a workshop on the demography of forced migration in 1998. The report of this workshop, published in 1999, summarized the field and suggested some potential directions for further research, as identified by participants.

As there was an obvious need for a vehicle for further exploration of these topics and others, the Committee on Population, with support from the Andrew W. Mellon Foundation, developed the Roundtable on the Demography of Forced Migration. The Roundtable provides a forum in which a diverse group of experts can discuss the state of knowledge about demographic structures and processes among people who are forced to move, whether to escape war and political violence, to flee famine and other natural disasters, or by government projects or programs that destroy their homes and communities. The Roundtable's task is often confounded by definitional problems (e.g., what is "forced migration"), and by a lack of data or data whose representativeness is unknown.

The Roundtable includes representatives from operational agencies, with long field and administrative experience. It includes researchers and scientists with both applied and scholarly experience in medicine, demography, and epidemiology. The group also includes representatives from government, international organizations, donors, universities, and non-governmental organizations. The Roundtable is organized to be as inclusive as possible of relevant expertise and to provide occasions for substantive sharing to increase knowledge for all participants with a view toward developing cumulative facts to inform policy and programs in complex humanitarian emergencies. The accomplishment of this goal will necessarily advance our knowledge about demographic structures and processes during and following high levels of social stress. This cannot help but enlighten demography as a field regarding comparative situations, such as famine, as well as provide contrasts to more "normal" social histories and the lives of people.

The first workshop organized by the Roundtable was on "Mortality Patterns in Complex Emergencies." Held in Washington, D.C., in November 1999, it was the first of a planned series of meetings attempting to survey what is known in the literature, what needs to be illuminated, and what current situations may tell us about the demography of current and future complex humanitarian emergencies. The objectives of the workshop were to explore patterns of mortality in recent crises and consider how these patterns resemble or differ from mortality in previous emergencies.

This volume emerges from the papers that were first presented at the workshop as well as the discussion at the workshop. It provides a basic overview of the state of knowledge about mortality in past complex humanitarian emergencies. Case studies on Rwanda, North Korea, and Kosovo, commissioned for the workshop, and on Cambodia, added after the workshop, provide focused reflection on complex emergencies as they have been in the past, as they are today, and as they appear to be for the near future.

The papers in this volume have been reviewed by individuals chosen for their diverse perspectives and technical expertise in accordance with procedures approved by the Report Review Committee of the National Research Council (NRC). The purpose of this independent review was to provide candid and critical comments that would assist the institution in making the published volume as accurate and as sound as possible and to ensure that it meets institutional standards for objectivity and evidence. The review comments and draft manuscripts remain confidential.

We thank the following individuals for their participation in the review of this volume: Richard Black, School of African and Asian Studies, University of Sussex; Allan G. Hill, Center for Population and Development Studies, School of Public Health, Harvard University; Jennifer Leaning, François-Xavier Bagnoud Center for Health and Human Rights, School of Public Health, Harvard University; Stephen Lubkemann, Watson Institute for International Studies, Brown University; M. Giovanna Merli, Department of Sociology, University of Wisconsin, Madison; Kathleen Newland, International Migration Policy Program, Carnegie Endowment for International Peace; Eric Noji, National Center for Infectious Diseases, Centers for Disease Control and Prevention; Susanne Schmeidl, Institute for Conflict Resolution, Swiss Peace Foundation; William Seltzer, Department of Sociology and Anthropology, Fordham University; and David Turton, Refugee Studies Centre, University of Oxford.

Although the individuals listed above have provided many constructive comments and suggestions, they were not asked to endorse the papers nor did they see the final drafts before publication. The review process was overseen by David Kertzer, Departments of Anthropology and History, Brown University. Appointed by the National Research Council, he was responsible for making certain that an independent examination of these papers was carried out in accordance with insitutional procedures and that all review comments were carefully considered. Responsibility for the final content of this volume rests entirely with the authors and editors of this volume.

We are also grateful to the staff and associates of the National Research Council. In particular, Holly Reed, who was instrumental in the organization of the workshop, coordinated the contributions of the au thors, co-authored the overview chapter, and coordinated the review process. Brian Tobachnick and Elizabeth Wallace expertly coordinated the logistical and travel arrangements for the workshop. Randi M. Blank edited the volume. Christine McShane guided the manuscript through the publication process and skillfully assisted with the editing. Sally Stanfield and the Audubon team at the National Academy Press handled the technical preparation of the report. Development and execution of this project occurred under the general guidance of the director of the Committee on Population, Barney Cohen.

We thank the Andrew W. Mellon Foundation, for its continual support of the work of the Roundtable as well as many others working in this field. A special thanks is due to Carolyn Makinson, Program Officer for Population and Forced Migration at the Mellon Foundation, for her enthusiasm and significant expertise in the field of forced migration. She has been an intellectual driving force behind the Roundtable's work.

We also wish to thank Charles Keely, of Georgetown University, a member of the Committee on Population and chair of the Roundtable, for his excellent work on the workshop and this volume, and his continued intellectual guidance for the Roundtable. Finally, we wish to recognize Ronald Waldman, of Columbia University, for his important substantive contributions in helping to organize the workshop.

Most of all, of course, we are grateful to the authors and other participants in the workshop, whose ideas have been captured in this volume. We hope that this publication helps to ensure the continuation of study about topics related to forced migration and ultimately contributes to both better policy and practice in the field.

Jane Menken
Chair, Committee on Population

Contents

1

Understanding Mortality Patterns in Complex Humanitarian Emergencies

Charles B. Keely, Holly E. Reed, and Ronald J. Waldman

The term *complex humanitarian emergency* is widely used to describe a particular type of disaster: a situation in which a large civilian population is affected by a combination of civil or international war, or a gross attempt to restructure the state or society (such as a genocide), leading to large-scale population displacement with accompanying deterioration of living conditions (such as food, potable water, shelter, and sanitation) creating the potential for a significant increase in mortality typically during some limited period of time, but sometimes lasting much longer.[1] Man-made complex humanitarian emergencies have existed throughout history. A small and arbitrary subset of examples includes events like the Roman attack on Carthage, the Goths' attack on Rome, and conquests by Islamic and Crusader forces. In the 20th century, complex humanitarian emergencies include the Holocaust in Europe in the 1930s and 1940s, the Bengal famine of 1943, and the murder or expulsion of the Chinese from Indonesia in the 1960s. Examples of complex humanitarian emergencies in even more recent years include wars, ethnic cleansing, forced migration, and genocide occurring in places as varied as Somalia, Bosnia, Rwanda, Kosovo, Sierra Leone, and East Timor.

One justification for a detailed review of mortality in such situations is the widespread assumption among the health and assistance communi-

---

[1] This definition is adapted from Toole and Waldman (1997). It has been somewhat modified to take a wider variety of complex humanitarian emergencies into account.

ties that "(t)he crude mortality rate (CMR) most accurately represents [in a single measure] the health status of emergency-affected populations" (Toole and Waldman, 1997). Mortality is indeed a valuable event to measure in emergencies; although it refers to only one dimension, it is a useful summary measure of the scale of the crisis and its impact, as well as the performance of those working to provide aid. Mortality estimates can be highly inaccurate, but they are often better and more easily captured than other health indicators, which may be subject to different definitions and cultural interpretations. There are many other potential outcomes of complex humanitarian emergencies, including morbidity, a possible change in fertility, migration, changes in family and household structures, broader societal changes, psychological effects, and potential cultural shifts. Mortality, however, has so far been one of the most easily and accurately measured indicators in an emergency setting. Since the mid-1980s, therefore, mortality rates have become a basic indicator in complex humanitarian emergencies (Hansch, 1999).

Concern for human life raises many questions about the causes, consequences, correlates, and measurement of mortality in complex humanitarian emergencies:

- How do mortality patterns differ in different kinds of complex humanitarian emergencies?
- How do mortality rates differ between refugee and internally displaced populations?
- How do mortality patterns differ in various types of geographic settings?
- How do mortality patterns differ by gender, age, or other groupings?
- How do mortality patterns in complex humanitarian emergencies differ from (or are similar to) "normal" mortality patterns?
- How does the distance traveled by refugees affect mortality?
- How does the length of a crisis affect mortality?
- How does food insecurity affect mortality? and
- What are the effects of various humanitarian interventions on mortality?

The case studies in this volume and the collected wisdom based on several decades of relief aid in emergencies provide a good starting point for understanding mortality patterns in complex humanitarian emergencies. However, much of this knowledge is based on data collected in camp settings and must be adapted for different situations. There are still many issues that remain unresolved and many new issues that must be examined. It is also important to realize the potential policy and program implications of such research. If researchers gain a better understanding of mortality patterns in emergencies and their underlying causes, then this may point to new interventions and/or improvements to current interventions that could reduce mortality in future emergencies. Many of the public health policies and recommendations that humanitarian assistance agencies use today are a direct result of the findings of research conducted in emergency settings in earlier decades.

This introductory overview presents some key definitions and a crude typology of complex humanitarian emergencies, summarizes current knowledge about mortality in complex humanitarian emergencies, outlines some of the new contexts that may affect complex emergencies, and discusses how data constraints affect existing knowledge. Finally, the contents of the volume are briefly previewed and some potential next steps are presented. We have also included an appendix of five case studies of mortality patterns in complex humanitarian emergencies, compiled by Steve Hansch. The appendix further illustrates some of the points made in this paper with reference to the difficulties of obtaining even rough estimates of mortality in complex humanitarian emergencies during or immediately following a crisis when assistance needs critically depend on these estimates. It may also serve to enrich some readers' understanding of the nature of complex humanitarian emergencies.

DEFINITIONS AND TYPOLOGY

Definitions

"A disaster may be defined as a relatively acute situation created by man-made, geophysical, weather-related, or biological events that adversely impacts on the health and economic well being of a community to an extent that exceeds the local coping capacity" (Toole and Waldman, 1997: 284). Complex humanitarian emergencies[2] are distinguished from acute natural disasters because population displacement and the lack of basic services available to a migrating population result in indirect or secondary health and mortality effects to a degree not usually present in a natural disaster. The disruption of services and life generally can often be addressed with some rapidity, especially if the population remains more or less in place. The difference between a complex emergency and a natural disaster is not necessarily in the mortality rate per se. Natural disasters can result in huge loss of life as a result of earthquake, weather,

---

[2] For the sake of brevity, the term "complex humanitarian emergency" will simply be "complex emergency" throughout the rest of the chapter.

or other natural causes. Complex emergencies, in addition to being caused by human beings, typically involve large-scale population displacements and the disruption of normal life to an extent that is beyond the means of typical coping mechanisms of a society. People may be displaced either within a country—internally displaced persons (IDPs)—or between one or more countries—refugees. It is the unusual and threatening conditions brought on by the disruption of society that lead to negative health and mortality consequences for such populations.

The concept *crude mortality rate* (CMR) is discussed frequently throughout the volume, which demographers often refer to as the *crude death rate* (CDR). The concept denotes the number of deaths in a given period of time divided by an estimate of the population at risk of dying during that period (Shryock and Siegel, 1976). In this chapter, we will refer to the number of deaths per 10,000 population per day as the daily crude mortality rate or CMR, and to the number of deaths per 1,000 population per year as the annual crude death rate or CDR. The two expressions are convertible by multiplying the CDR (more familiar to demographers) by 36.5 to obtain the CMR (more familiar to epidemiologists working in complex emergency situations).

Baseline mortality is the "normal" mortality level in a given population. Epidemiologists often refer to a "return to baseline level," which indicates a stabilization of the situation and potential end to the mortality crisis. However, with refugee or internally displaced populations, it is often difficult to define the baseline, because the population of comparison may not be clearly defined, populations may have chronically high mortality rates due to ongoing conflict and other problems, and surveillance may have started well into the period of elevated mortality.

Typology

Grouping various complex emergencies into distinct categories may help emergency aid organizations to identify the types of assistance that are most likely to be needed early in a crisis. One such typology distinguishes between five types of crises based on their settings and patterns of population risk (Hansch, 1999).

• *Rural Famine or Refugee Paradigm:* This is the model on which most relief work has traditionally been based. Populations are expected to be rural, poor, and illiterate, with low vaccination coverage and high chronic malnutrition, and they are generally housed in high-density camps. Mortality is often due to communicable diseases compounded by malnutrition. Deaths generally occur disproportionately among children less than five years of age. Examples of this type of crisis include: Biafra, Nigeria, in 1968; the Sahel in 1973, and Sudan, Ethiopia, and Somalia in the late 1980s and early 1990s.

  • *Ethnic Cleansing or Genocide:* This type is increasingly common and is characterized by armed forces (sometimes assisted by civilians) attacking large numbers of civilians in an effort to kill or displace them. Mortality is due in large part, if not mainly, to physical injury, not communicable diseases or malnutrition. Disability and mental health trauma are other important consequences of this type of emergency. Examples of this type of emergency include: Rwanda in 1994; Bosnia in the early 1990s, and Kosovo in 1999.

  • *Urban Services Collapse or Urban Depopulation:* This type of crisis occurs when generally healthy and well-nourished populations who are dependent on urban services become refugees due to war. Mortality is usually due to chronic diseases and lack of sophisticated health systems (i.e., kidney dialysis machines). This type of crisis has occurred within larger crises in Somalia, Bosnia, and Kosovo.

  • *Conflict Among Combatants:* Most mortality occurs among armed combatants due to battle injuries, landmines, collateral damage, or communicable diseases associated with the effects of war. This type of emergency includes: Cambodia and Angola in the 1980s and 1990s (where landmines were a significant mortality risk) and Chechnya.

  • *Short-Onset, Short-Duration Natural Disaster:* Hurricanes, tornadoes, and earthquakes can create high mortality rates at the beginning of a crisis based on physical trauma or environmental exposure. However, these types of disasters can lead to longer-term problems such as famine and disease if they are not addressed immediately. Examples include: floods in Bangladesh and earthquakes in Mexico and South America. This type of emergency is not discussed in detail in this volume because it is generally caused more by natural than political factors.

Clearly, these categories are rarely completely distinct and often overlap, but may be useful in a debate about how the nature of complex emergencies are evolving over time (see below).

CURRENT KNOWLEDGE

Extent of the Problem

Although complex emergencies have been occurring for centuries, systematic data on the numbers of forced migrants in the world have only been available for approximately the past 40 years. The number of refugees and IDPs in the world has increased dramatically during the past four decades. As Figure 1-1 shows, by the end of 1998, there were over

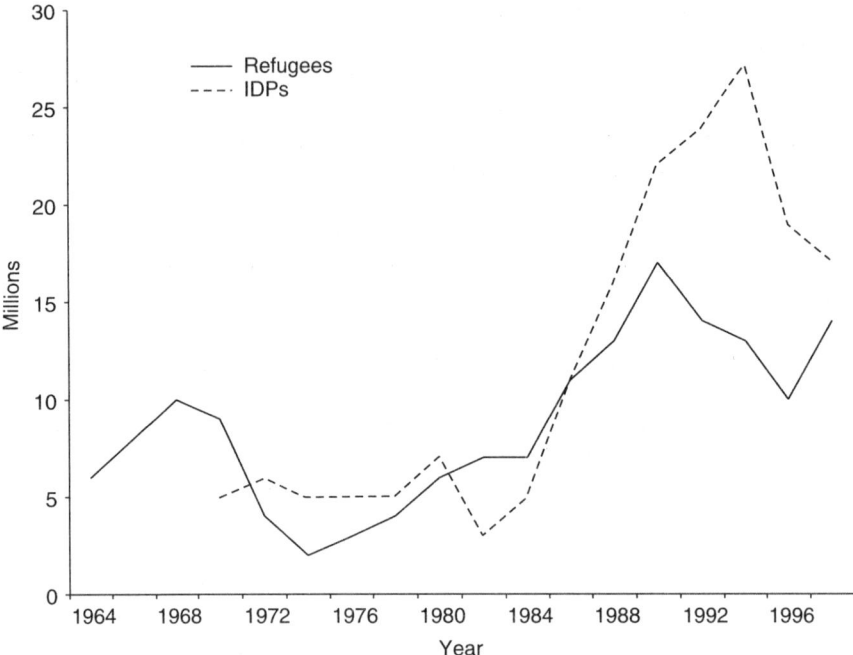

FIGURE 1-1   Global trends in refugees and internally displaced persons, 1964-1999. United States Committee for Refugees and United Nations High Commissioner for Refugees, various years.

11.6 million refugees, almost twice as many as there were 36 years ago. Yet in recent years, since about 1991, the number of refugees has generally declined, despite a brief rise in the late 1990s (United Nations High Commissioner for Refugees, 2000). Meanwhile, the number of IDPs has grown quite rapidly, reaching over 25 million by 1994, although this figure also declined slightly in the late 1990s to about 17 million by 1998. The map that follows page 18 shows that, refugees and internally displaced persons are located around the globe—in Africa, Central and South America, Eastern Europe, the Middle East, and Central and Southern Asia (United States Committee for Refugees, 2000). Due to the political nature of flows of refugees and internally displaced persons, one must acknowledge not only the effect of global and local political events, but also the willingness of states and international organizations to count persons as refugees and IDPs. This varies with circumstances; therefore, interpretations of trends in the number of forced migrants require caution.

Although not every refugee or IDP in the world is currently affected by a complex emergency, complex emergencies do produce forced migrants. The number of complex emergencies has also increased over the past decade. In 1989, there were 14 ongoing emergencies; in 1992, there were 17. By 1996, there were 24 ongoing complex emergencies in the world, and there were about 30 by the end of 1999 (Natsios, 1997; United States Committee for Refugees, 2000). However, the realignment of state boundaries and the creation of additional states in places such as the former Soviet Union and former Yugoslavia may have some effect on these statistics. This apparent increase in emergencies has been accompanied by a parallel increase in emergency foreign aid expenditures by the United States. In 1989, the U.S. spent $300 million in bilateral aid for foreign disasters and crises. By 1994, it was spending $1.3 billion. There is a corresponding trend in multilateral expenditures for emergency assistance. Between 1984 and 1989, for example, the World Food Program spent 25 to 40 percent of its annual assistance budget on relief activities. By 1992-1993, this was up to over 60 percent (Natsios, 1997). However, it is important to note that an increase in emergency foreign aid does not necessarily translate into an increase in overall foreign aid.

Levels of Mortality

In complex emergencies, the crude mortality rate (CMR) is often expressed as the number of deaths per 10,000 population per day during the acute phase of an emergency. Calculating a daily rate has been considered to be appropriate since conditions can change dramatically on a daily basis and the large base of 10,000 per day is used to express events in whole numbers. In developing countries, the median crude death rate (CDR) for the total population is 9 deaths per 1,000 per year (Population Reference Bureau, 2000). This translates into a daily rate of 0.25 deaths per 10,000. A threshold of 1.0 per 10,000 per day is widely used as the benchmark of elevated mortality, on the recommendation of the Centers for Disease Control and Prevention (1992). This threshold of 1 per 10,000 per day is equivalent to an annual CDR of 36.5 per 1,000.[3]

---

[3] Throughout the rest of this chapter, the term *crude death rate (CDR)* will be used to refer to a rate of deaths per 1,000 population per year, while the term *crude mortality rate (CMR)* will be used to refer to a rate of deaths per 10,000 population per day. It should be noted, however, that although the threshold CMR of 1 death per 10,000 per day is widely used, it is unclear how elevated this really is. Mortality in the early stages is most likely to affect vulnerable groups like the chronically ill, the malnourished, and the population under five years of age. Since CMRs are calculated for the whole population, they do not show decomposition by age groups. If mortality is to a large extent confined to the under-five population, and if deaths take place within the first months after flight, then a return to baseline mortality measured as a CMR may indicate that the surviving population has achieved mortality rates lower than the pre-flight levels. For example, in Baidoa, Somalia,

Although the CMR and CDR are essentially the same concept, there are reasons for preferring to use one rather than the other. Demographers have traditionally favored longer reference periods for demographic rates as they are generally interested in average mortality over a period of time. Epidemiologists working in emergencies, however, are interested in the "instantaneous" rate. Therefore they use the daily rate (CDR)[4] to observe rapid changes in the mortality rate which shows whether or not the situation is stabilizing.

Elevated CMRs in complex emergencies vary widely. Table 1-1, based on data in Toole and Waldman (1997) provides a dozen examples of CMRs and CDRs expressed in terms of daily rates per 10,000 and annual rates per 1,000. The table has the virtue of providing information on emergencies in different parts of the world around the same time period, as well as estimates for some of the same countries at different times and estimates for refugee populations from the same origin country in different asylum countries.

The data shown in Table 1-1 indicate a daily CMR on a base of 10,000 of over 1 in all of the cases given. The range is between 1.2 in the case of Mozambicans in Malawi in June 1992 to some of the highest levels ever measured—between 19.4 to 30.9 deaths per 10,000 per day at the height of the Rwandan crisis in July 1994. The Rwandan levels, if sustained, would have meant that every refugee would have been dead in less than a year. (The level of 1,127.9 per 1,000 per year means annihilation in less than a year.)

The heavy reliance on data collected from camp populations may distort understanding of the levels and trends of mortality among the total refugee and internally displaced populations. Camp populations may benefit from earlier and more effective assistance interventions that lead to a reversal of the high mortality levels associated with the emergency and result in a more quickly stabilized situation in terms of food,

---

in 1992, about 75 percent of children under five years of age died in a six-month period and the percentage of children under five years of age in the population dropped from 18.3 percent to 7.8 percent (Moore et al., 1993). However, an occurrence like this does not change the life expectancy for survivors; it means that those who were at the greatest risk of dying have already died, and therefore the mortality rate may be lower than it was before the emergency. It may also be possible that the provision of food, shelter, sanitation, immunizations, and basic primary care may increase the life expectancy for the remaining population and therefore, result in lower mortality rates for survivors compared to their baseline experience. In any such event this must be offset by the traumatic experiences suffered by these populations during war, famine, flight, and refuge.

[4] Note that the so-called "daily" rate may not actually be a daily rate as it is often based on the average mortality experience over a number of days. It still gives a sense of the mortality levels in relatively "real time," however.

TABLE 1-1 Estimated Daily Crude Mortality Rates (CMRs) and Annual Crude Death Rates (CDRs) in Selected Refugee Populations, 1990-1994

Date	Asylum Country	Origin Country	Daily CMR[a]	Annual CDR[b]
July 1990	Ethiopia	Sudan	2.3	84.0
June 1991	Ethiopia	Somalia	4.6	167.9
March-May 1991	Turkey	Iraq	4.1	149.7
March-May 1991	Iran	Iraq	2.0	73.0
March 1992	Kenya	Somalia	7.3	266.5
March 1992	Nepal	Bhutan	3.0	109.5
June 1992	Bangladesh	Burma	1.6	58.4
June 1992	Malawi	Mozambique	1.2	43.8
August 1992	Zimbabwe	Mozambique	3.5	127.8
December 1993	Rwanda	Burundi	3.0	109.5
August 1994	Tanzania	Rwanda	3.0	109.5
July 1994	Zaire	Rwanda	19.4-30.9	708.1-1,127.9

[a]Expressed as deaths per 10,000 per day.
[b]Expressed as deaths per 1,000 per year.
Source: Toole and Waldman (1997: Table 2)

shelter, sanitation, and other basic needs. On the other hand, camp situations may increase the risk of subsequent mortality due to infectious diseases. Although delivering assistance in camps may be more manageable for providers, it may not be more effective for recipients. Under certain circumstances, self-settlement among a host population may be more effective (Van Damme, 1995).

Complex emergencies rarely continue indefinitely. In most cases, international organizations, national governments, nongovernmental organizations, and others intervene to provide some stability for the refugee population, and minimal services are aimed at reduction of mortality, reduction of morbidity, and other threats to life. What the data in Table 1-1 underscore is that the acuteness of the challenge, as indicated by CMRs, varies enormously from situation to situation.

Internally displaced persons, who often face the same difficult survival conditions as refugees who have crossed an international border, also face the prospect of elevated mortality. Because of considerations of sovereignty and the absence of international agreements about the provision of protection and assistance to victims of persecution and war who remain in their own country, internally displaced persons are less likely to receive international assistance that might meet survival needs and provide a modicum of stability. Although mortality data on internally displaced populations are scarce, most of the situations for which data are available display very high mortality rates. As shown in Table 1-2, the

TABLE 1-2   Estimated Daily Crude Mortality Rates (CMRs) and Annual Crude Death Rates (CDRs) Among Internally Displaced Persons, 1990-1994

Date	Country	Daily CMR[a]	Annual CDR[b]
January-December 1990	Liberia	2.3	84.0
April 1991-March 1992	Somalia (Merca)	4.5	164.3
April-November 1992	Somalia (Baidoa)	16.7	609.6
April-December 1992	Somalia (Afgoi)	5.4	197.1
April 1992-March 1993	Sudan (Ayod)	7.6	277.4
April 1992-March 1993	Sudan (Akon)	4.5	164.3
April 1992-March 1993	Bosnia (Zepa)	1.0	36.5
April 1993	Bosnia (Sarajevo)	1.0	36.5
May 1995	Angola (Cafunfo)	8.2	299.3
February 1996	Liberia (Bong)	5.4	197.1

[a]Expressed as deaths per 10,000 per day.
[b]Expressed as deaths per 1,000 per year.
Source: Adapted from Toole and Waldman (1997: Table 3).

CMR in Baidoa, Somalia, in 1992 was almost 17 deaths per 10,000 per day and in both Sudan in 1992-1993 and Angola in 1995, it was over 7 per 10,000 per day. Crude mortality rates among Muslims in Bosnia during the war in 1993 were about four times the baseline level (Toole et al., 1993).

Stages of a Crisis

The data in Table 1-1 highlight the degree to which mortality can rise in crisis situations but reveal nothing about patterns of mortality over the various stages of a particular complex emergency. Each complex emergency is typically different from the last: different logistics, different politics, different social context, etc. However, some generalizations are possible. Figure 1-2 shows the classic rural famine/refugee paradigm pattern, which is a refinement of an inverted U-shaped pattern. Note the sharp increase at the beginning of the crisis (Phase 1), followed by the peak mortality rate (Phase 2) and then a relatively rapid decline (Phase 3), and stabilization (Phase 4). These distinctions should be based not so much on absolute measurements, but on patterns. In other words, in an emergency, population parameters—including mortality—may be quite unstable—either fluctuating or rapidly changing due to interventions or other reasons. The post-emergency phase is usually marked by more stable mortality rates, even though they might remain unacceptably el-

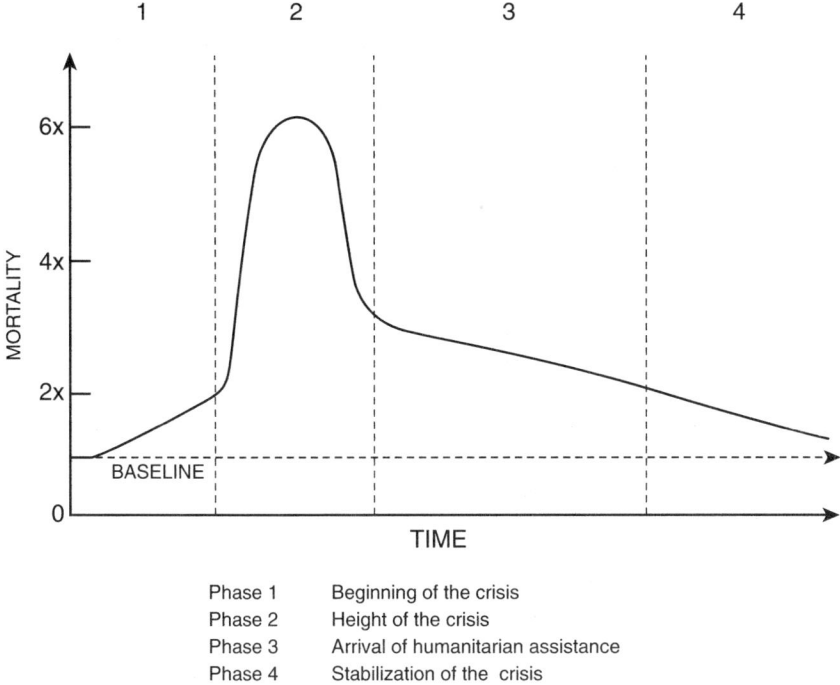

FIGURE 1-2   Model of mortality change in a forced migration situation. Source: Reed et al., 1998, Figure 2.

evated. However, stabilization is what signals the time to shift programming from life-saving interventions to longer-term ones.

Typically, the period of flight and the time immediately after arrival in a place of asylum are the periods of highest mortality. In 1992, in Chambuta camp, Zimbabwe, for example, Mozambican refugees who had been in the camp for less than one month had a CMR of 8 per 10,000, which was four times that of those who had been in the camp for one to three months and 16 times the baseline (Centers for Disease Control and Prevention, 1993a). In Goma, Zaire, among Rwandan refugees, the average daily CMR from July 14 to August 14, 1994, was between 19.5 and 31.2 per 10,000. This was more than 30 times the baseline rate (Goma Epidemiology Group, 1995).

The rate at which mortality rates decline varies across populations, and the speed of mortality reduction also depends on the rates of mortality and/or out-migration of specific groups at high risk for mortality. For example, the initial high mortality rates of Cambodian refugees in Thailand in 1979 declined to baseline levels in about one month (Toole and

Waldman, 1990). In Goma, Zaire, among Rwandan refugees, nearly 2,000 deaths per day were estimated on July 21, 1994, but by July 28, there were over 6,500 deaths per day. By August 4, the number of deaths per day was less than 1,000 (Goma Epidemiology Group, 1995). Although this is still a large number of deaths, the acuteness of the crisis moderated with some rapidity. Other situations, however, are much harder to stabilize, usually because of political factors. In 1988-1989, for example, under-five mortality among Somali refugees in Ethiopia remained high for about 18 months, even increasing during some periods (Toole and Bhatia, 1992).

It is important to note that this model does not hold true for all complex emergencies and it has not been systematically validated. It is simply an approximation of mortality patterns that have been observed in many of these situations in the past. Although it is possible to speculate about the factors that cause a shift in the mortality pattern, it is impossible to generalize and often very difficult to measure.

Sometimes it is quite clear why variations in mortality patterns occur, but generally the relative impact of variables like age and sex composition, proportions and types of vulnerable groups, levels of mortality among vulnerable groups early in an emergency, and other factors is unknown. However, one reason for the variation in the speed of the mortality reduction is obviously the promptness of assistance efforts. How promptly assistance is provided is a function of many factors, including awareness of the situation, political decisions about whether or not to assist, ease of access to the displaced population, vulnerability of the population (because of the conditions and length of their flight), prior health status of the population, and reported mortality rates (among the most vulnerable). Although the general pattern is one of elevated mortality, followed by rapid declines with the arrival of assistance and a modicum of stable and safe living conditions, there is wide variation in the rapidity of mortality declines and improvement in the health and living conditions of refugee populations.

Reasons for Elevated Risk of Mortality in Complex Emergencies

It is too easy to overlook what are usually the initial direct causes of mortality and the underlying causes for all other mortality in a complex emergency. Violence from war and starvation due to famine kill many civilians directly and are often the reasons for flight which results in refugees and internally displaced persons. The root of most complex humanitarian emergencies is that governments and other combatants use violence and deprivation to seek solutions for political problems.

Violence is a major cause of mortality in complex emergencies. Armed conflicts, both civil wars and transnational conflicts, have increasingly targeted civilians. High numbers of civilian dead, human rights abuses, forced migration, and socioeconomic breakdown have been the result. In addition, injuries from war and landmines are common, particularly among IDPs (Toole and Waldman, 1997). For example, between April 1992 and January 1993 in Sarajevo, Bosnia, 57 percent of all mortality was due to war trauma (Centers for Disease Control and Prevention, 1993b).

Food scarcity, especially if experienced by a population with already elevated levels of malnutrition, can also lead to elevated mortality in complex emergencies. The same is true of lack of access to water. Malnutrition and dehydration can quickly increase mortality rates in a population, especially one in an already weakened state. Data on 42 different refugee populations between 1984 and 1988 showed a strong positive correlation between the acute protein energy malnutrition (PEM) prevalence and crude mortality rates. Populations with low PEM prevalence rates (less than 5 percent) had a low average monthly CDR (0.9 per 1,000 per month). But those populations with PEM prevalence rates of at least 40 percent had an average CDR of 37 per 1,000 (Person-Karell, 1989). In 1988-1989, among Somali refugees in Eastern Ethiopia, malnutrition prevalence and the CDR were also found to be positively correlated (Centers for Disease Control and Prevention, 1990).

There are many correlates to these causes of mortality, however. Displacement itself, because of the often-harsh conditions and long duration of flight, may be related to mortality. Deprivations during the ordeal, additional dangers encountered along the way, and lengthy disruption of ordinary life put great direct physical stress on people and also indirectly affect health status through physical and psychological stress that may increase their vulnerability to health problems and the levels of mortality. Thus refugees are often at the highest risk for mortality immediately after they arrive in a host country (Toole and Waldman, 1997).

Weakened populations are also more vulnerable to disease. During the early phases of an emergency, diarrheal diseases (e.g., cholera, dysentery), measles, acute respiratory infections, and malaria are the most common causes of death (Toole and Waldman, 1997). Among Rwandan refugees in Zaire in 1994, over 90 percent of deaths within the first month of the crisis were attributable to a severe cholera epidemic followed by a dysentery outbreak (Goma Epidemiology Group, 1995). Before 1990, measles epidemics were quite common in many refugee settings and led to large numbers of deaths in Somalia, Bangladesh, Sudan, and Ethiopia (Toole et al., 1989). However, since that time, immunization campaigns have reduced this threat somewhat. Malaria is often a problem in tropical areas such as Southeast Asia and sub-Saharan Africa. Other diseases that frequently attack refugees include acute respiratory infections, meningitis, hepatitis, tuberculosis, and HIV and other sexually transmitted diseases (Toole and Waldman, 1997).

A collapse of or lack of health services can also contribute to increased mortality. The breakdown of health services, particularly preventive services such as immunization and prenatal care, is often due to a combination of infrastructure collapse, economic failure, and lack of resources for public services. Personnel and equipment shortages exacerbated by the challenge of treating countless war casualties can overwhelm health systems (Toole and Waldman, 1997). Again, the multiplier effect of more than one element is evident in the particular risk of increases in communicable diseases if there is a combination of bad living conditions and a collapse of health services (Noji, 1997).

The Age Pattern of Mortality in Complex Emergencies

Another factor that contributes to elevated mortality in complex emergencies is the presence of vulnerable groups in the population. Those who are already at highest risk are going to be even more vulnerable during times of displacement and deprivation. The leading causes of death in refugee situations (with the exception of direct violence leading to death) are the same killers encountered in ordinary situations, and those who are most vulnerable in refugee situations are generally the same persons who are vulnerable under normal circumstances.

Risk clearly varies by age. For example, in 1980, in one camp in Somalia for Ethiopian refugees, daily mortality rates for those younger than five during the emergency phase were 28 per 10,000, much higher than for adults (Toole and Waldman, 1988). In 1985, under-age-five mortality rates among Ethiopian and Eritrean refugees in some Sudanese camps were one and a half times the CMR (Toole and Waldman, 1988). And among displaced Iraqis on the Turkey-Iraq border in March to May 1991, children under five years of age made up over 63 percent of all deaths (Centers for Disease Control and Prevention, 1991). Again, this pattern of mortality is quite similar to the normal circumstances in many developing countries.

In more developed regions, however, the elderly are often at greater risk. For example, in Sarajevo, Bosnia, from December 1993 to March 1994, elderly residents and refugees were found to be a particularly vulnerable group to malnutrition and its effects. The percentage of adults 60 years and older who were undernourished during these four months was over 15 percent, which was over three times the percentage of undernourishment in the rest of the population (Watson et al., 1995).

A more sophisticated question, however, is to ask how does the shape of the mortality pattern in complex emergencies differ from the underlying mortality pattern pre-existing in a stable population. By comparing age-specific mortality rates in emergencies to those occurring in a hypothetical stable population with a similar life expectancy, researchers can

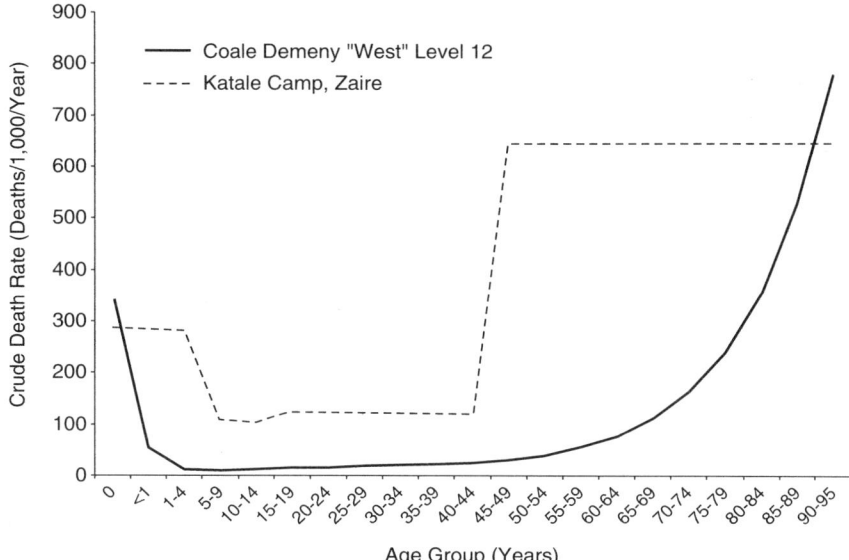

FIGURE 1-3   Age-specific death rates for Rwandan refugees in Katale Camp, Zaire, July 17-August 5, 1994 and for Coale-Demeny life table "West" level 12.

determine how the relative mortality risk differs for different age groups during an emergency. Few data on age-specific mortality in emergencies exist, but it is possible to analyze the data that can be found. We have analyzed data for three different emergencies by comparing them to age-specific mortality rates from relevant Coale-Demeny West life tables. In each of these graphs, one can observe the typical "J-shaped" mortality pattern of the Coale-Demeny curve, with the highest death rates occurring in the youngest and oldest ages (Coale et al., 1983).

In Figure 1-3, the age-specific mortality pattern for a Coale-Demeny "West" Level 12 life table with an average life expectancy of about 45.5 years[5] is compared to the mortality pattern among Rwandan refugees living in Katale Camp, Zaire, in the summer of 1994 (Davis, 1996). Although only data for broad age groups were collected in the camp (and therefore the curve is incomplete and not very smooth), the general pattern is similar to the Coale-Demeny curve. Mortality is extremely elevated in the youngest and oldest age groups, compared to the middle ages. Mortality at most ages appears to be significantly higher than for the stable population.

---

[5] According to the 1994 World Development Report, the average life expectancy at birth for Rwanda in 1992 was 46 years. No estimates are available for the years 1993, 1994 (World Bank, 1994; World Bank, 1995; World Bank, 1996).

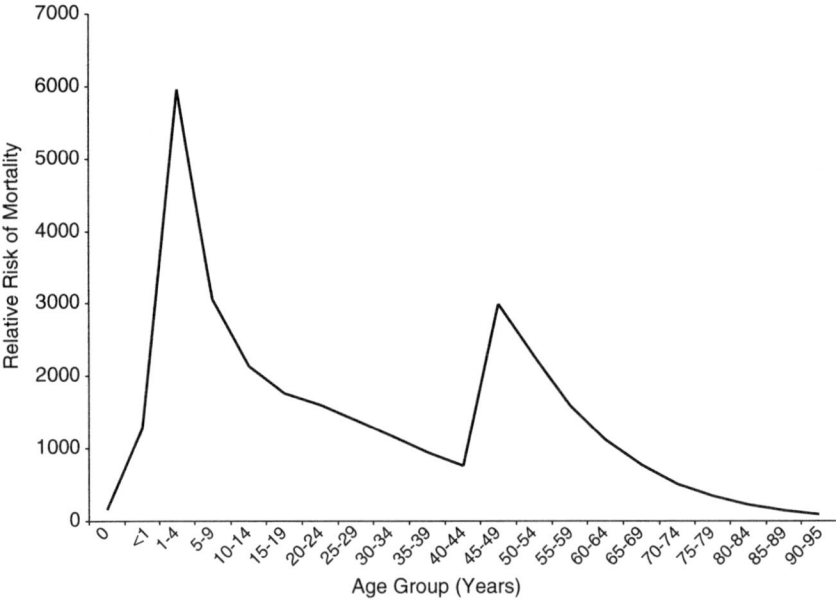

FIGURE 1-4   Relative risk of mortality for Rwandan refugees in Katale Camp, Zaire, July 17-August 5, 1994 compared to risk of mortality for stable population based on Coale-Demeny life table "West" level 12.

Figure 1-4 shows the relative risk of dying in the Rwandan refugee camp compared to the risk of dying for a stable population with a life expectancy of 45.5 years at birth (approximately the same as that for the population of Rwanda before the 1994 crisis). All age groups have an elevated risk of mortality, but some are enormously high. Children aged 1 to 4 are 6000 percent more likely to die in the refugee camp compared to the stable population. Adults aged 45-49 also had high risk of mortality; they were about 3000 percent more likely to die compared to the same group in the stable population. It is known that cholera and shigella were the main causes of disease in this camp. It is not surprising that young children were quite vulnerable to these epidemics. The large risk of death for adults may also be related to the waves of disease (Davis, 1996).

Figures 1-5 and 1-6 compare male age-specific mortality in a long-term Cambodian refugee camp in Thailand to a Coale-Demeny West Level 14 male life table with a life expectancy of about 49.5 years[6] (Elias et al., 1990). In Figure 1-5, mortality appears to be only slightly elevated among

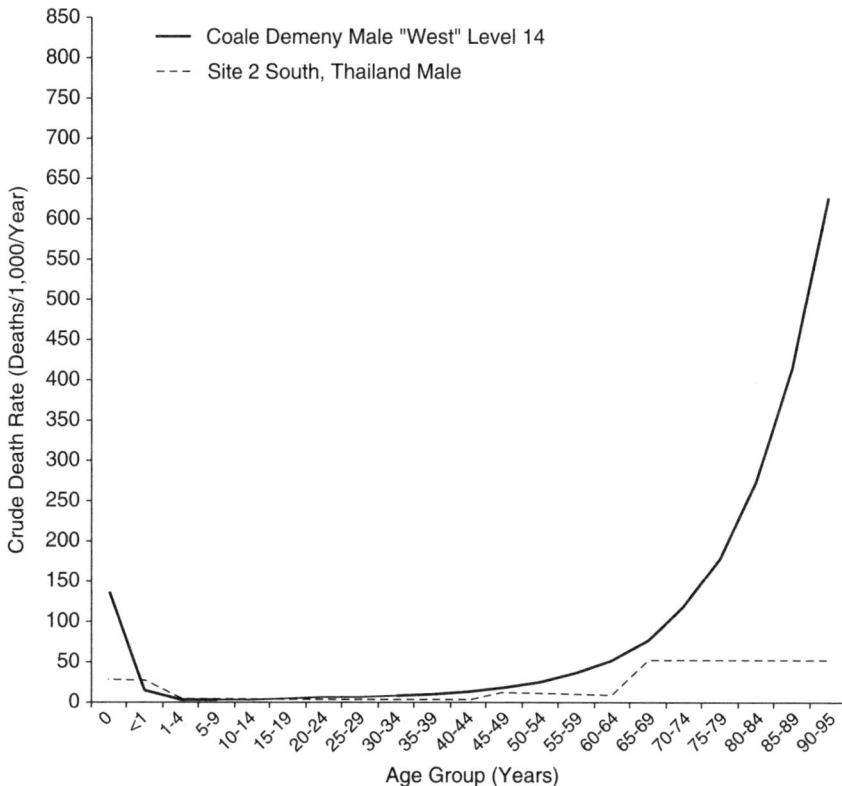

FIGURE 1-5 Age-specific death rates for male Cambodian refugees in Thailand, June 1987-May 1988 and for Coale-Demeny life table "West" level 14, males.

the older and younger age groups. As Figure 1-6 shows, however, the relative risk of dying is over 80 percent greater for male refugees under one year of age compared to the same age group in the stable population. Mortality risk for the rest of the male refugee population is lower than for the stable population. These data demonstrate the stark difference between the crisis of the Rwandan refugee camp and the relatively reduced mortality risk found in a long-term stable refugee camp that was in existence for over 10 years in Thailand.

---

[6] According to the 1992 World Development Report, the average life expectancy at birth for Cambodia (Democratic Republic of Kampuchea) in 1990 was 50 years. No estimate is available for the year 1989 (World Bank, 1991; World Bank, 1992).

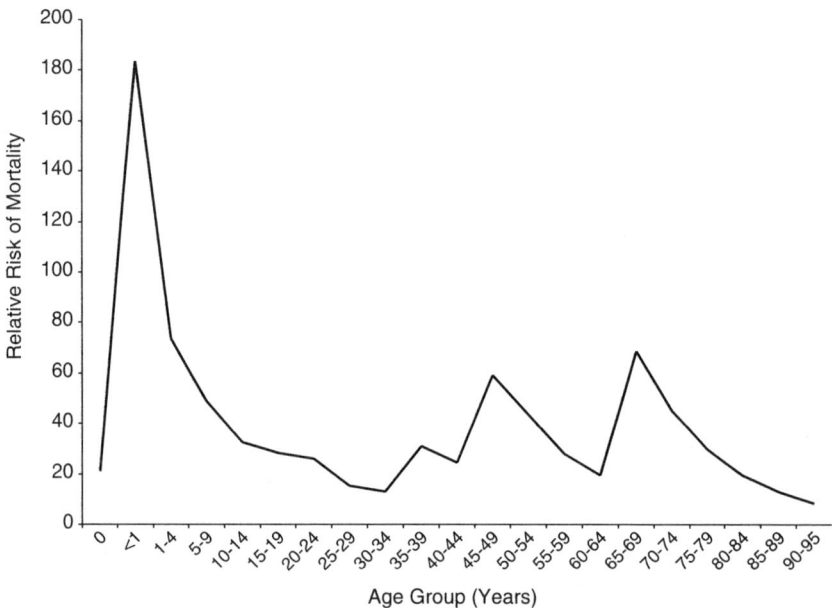

FIGURE 1-6   Relative risk of mortality for male Cambodian refugees in Thailand, June 1987-May 1988 compared to risk of mortality for stable population based on Coale-Demeny life table "West" level 14, male.

Figures 1-7 and 1-8 compare female age-specific mortality in the same Cambodian refugee camp to a Coale-Demeny West Level 14 female life table with a life expectancy of about 52.5 years.   In Figure 1-7, again mortality appears to be only slightly elevated among the older and younger age groups.   In Figure 1-8, however, again the mortality risk for those under one year of age is elevated and almost 20 percent greater compared to the same age group in the stable population.   Mortality risk for the rest of the female refugee population is also lower than for the stable population.

Within this volume, both Robinson et al. (Chapter 3) and Heuveline (Chapter 5) take a closer look at age-specific mortality rates in emergency settings.   In the North Korea study by Robinson et al. (see Figure 3-1), mortality rates for their sample are somewhat similar to those from the Coale-Demeny "West" Level 4 life table, although elevated in the younger and older ages and reduced in the middle ages.   Both of these curves show mortality levels much higher than those estimated by the 1993 North Korean census.

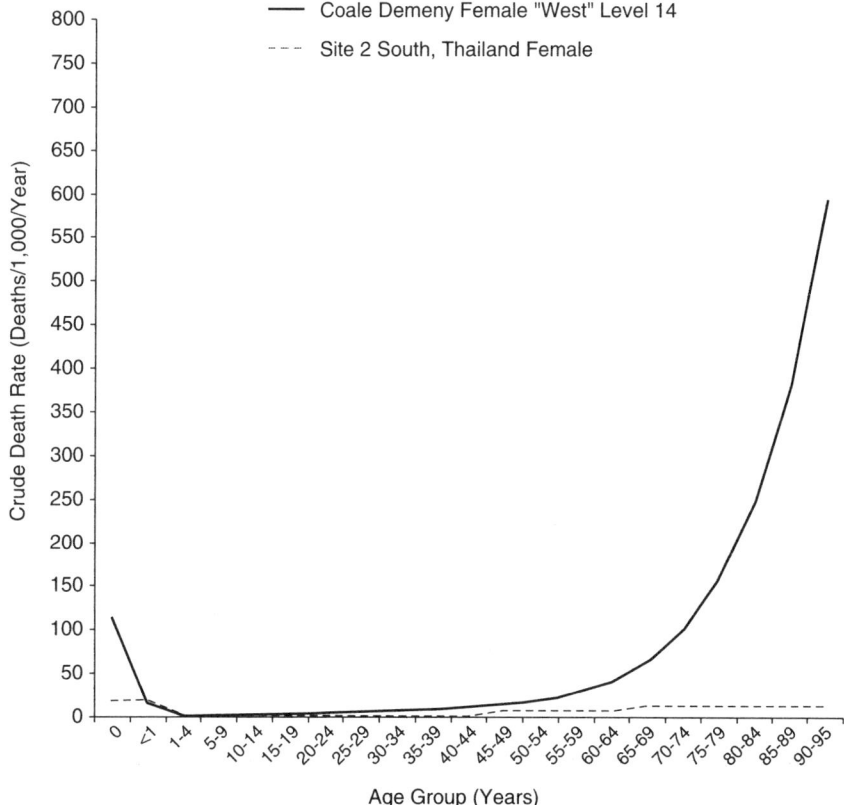

FIGURE 1-7 Age-specific death rates for female Cambodian refugees in Thailand, June 1987-May 1988 and for Coale-Demeny life table "West" level 14, females.

In Cambodia (see Figure 5-4), Heuveline found that deaths from natural causes followed the typical J-shaped curve for both men and women. Deaths from violent causes, however, had a completely different age and sex pattern. Men were much more likely to be killed in the younger age groups, from about age 5 to age 24 years, but has a lower probability of dying thereafter. Women, on the other hand, had a much lower probability of death due to violent causes, but the groups that were most vulnerable were very young women (under age 10) and women between the ages of 40 and 64.

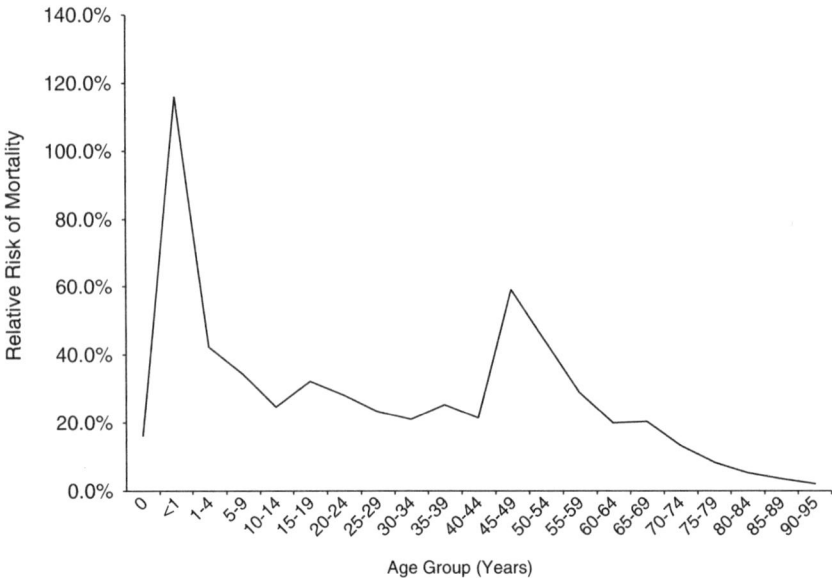

FIGURE 1-8   Relative risk of mortality for female Cambodian refugees in Thailand, June 1987-May 1988 compared to risk of mortality for stable population based on Coale-Demeny life table "West" level 14, female.

How Can Excess Mortality Be Reduced in a Complex Emergency?

The basic mechanisms to reduce excess mortality in complex emergencies are widely agreed upon in the emergency assistance community and are based on many years of experience. The first requirements are to provide a stable situation that allows the displaced persons to stop moving; to be free from violence; and to have access to nutritious food, clean water, adequate sanitation and shelter, and basic health services, of which the important aspect is often measles immunizations (Sphere Project, 2000). Note that the requirements to reduce mortality include only one primarily medical intervention: measles vaccination. What refugees need is a reduction in the physical demands of flight and then access to the ordinary means of human survival. The provision of food, water, shelter, and sanitation allows people to live, to regain strength, and to be protected from common communicable diseases. Protection from measles is also important because children who are in weakened condition are quite vulnerable to measles.

In addition to this basic list of provisions, some situations may require attention to specific environmental hazards. A frequent example is malaria. If malaria is present, a refugee population is likely to be more than usually vulnerable. In this case, it is important to implement environmental prevention methods, such as removing any stagnant water that attracts mosquitoes, distributing bed nets to the refugees, and possibly spraying the area with mosquito repellants. Other environmental hazards, including other insects and rodents, may require different interventions.

A third component that is necessary in refugee situations is the early establishment of a surveillance system to monitor the health of the population and detect early signs of emerging problems. Although in some instances surveillance systems are already in existence (early warning mechanisms, for example), if displaced populations are in remote or undeveloped areas, it is usually necessary to implement a system immediately. Surveillance systems can utilize community health workers from the affected refugee population. This requires training, but it may have positive externalities such as community involvement and increased knowledge about health conditions among the population.[7]

Finally, efforts to create new health services or supplement existing services can be a useful tool to address ordinary health issues as they arise in refugee situations, such as accidents, pregnancy, or other issues. In addition to basic survival needs, providing primary care services, addressing specific environmental risks (e.g., malaria), and establishing a working surveillance system should bring mortality rates back to base levels relatively quickly.

Knowing what to do in an emergency, however, does not minimize the difficulty of achieving these goals under field conditions. At times, the challenges of logistics are enormous, sometimes exacerbated by combatants' attempts to disrupt assistance. What is clear from a review of the literature is the confidence, based on repeated experiences, that the international assistance community knows how to reduce mortality to preflight baseline levels and maintain these levels (Waldman and Martone, 1999). Persistent excess mortality in a complex emergency is not the result of ignorance about effective procedures, but usually the result of extraordinary difficulties in the logistics of access to the refugees, interference of combatants, or the failure of the international community to provide sufficient resources.

---

[7] The recent experience of scholars who have reconstructed a record of human rights abuses and murder for criminal tribunals and truth commissions in widely dispersed locations underscores the need for utmost care to protect persons on whom information is collected. In this regard, surveillance system administrators need to address the issue of safety and confidentiality of record systems. Discussion between surveillance administrators, statisticians, and demographers conducting forensic research to establish records of events may help to create models for institutionalizing safeguards for record keeping in emergencies.

NEW CONTEXTS FOR COMPLEX EMERGENCIES

Having provided a brief overview of current knowledge on mortality in crisis situations, we now turn to the critical question of whether the nature and scope of complex emergencies are changing over time and how. There are many facets of today's complex emergencies that deserve attention: the shifting geopolitical map, a changing epidemiological context, new actors and new roles for older actors, increasing attention to the quality of relief, and a growing appreciation of information needs. All of these issues have important implications for the understanding of mortality patterns in crisis situations.

The Shifting Geopolitical Map

The end of the Cold War marked the beginning of a new geopolitical context for complex emergencies. In some cases, the withdrawal of U.S. or Soviet support has led to a destabilization of developing country governments. In addition, many conflicts that were previously exacerbated by the involvement of the United States and the Soviet Union are now regional or internal conflicts. On the other hand, however, there are no longer two distinct ideological camps that create barriers to resolving conflicts or prevent assistance interventions for fear of reprisal.

In the past, intervention on behalf of forced migrants was often due to ideological considerations, rather than simply humanitarian concern. The Eastern Bloc countries were not part of the international refugee regime, but produced many refugees of their own who were given automatic asylum in the West. Now these countries are not necessarily producing refugees (with the exception of the Balkan region), but they are hosting them. And migrants who do leave Eastern Europe and the former Soviet Union are much less likely to gain asylum in Western Europe or the United States (Rogers and Copeland, 1993).

Along with this change, there is a continuing transformation of the concept of sovereignty. There appears to be a more rapid and more controversial change process than occurred in the past. Many see an erosion of the concept, implying a negative shift in global political structure and practice. Others see greater transparency and accountability demanded of states and thus a positive development for the human, civic, and social rights of people. Globalization and the integration of economies, the media, the environment, and human rights have increasingly encroached upon traditional understandings of sovereignty in today's world. Many of these forces, in turn, have expanded the concept of security to include non-military issues. One consequence of this expanded notion of security is that refugee flows are viewed as a security threat

(Abiri, 2000; Wæver et al., 1993). Some national governments feel so threatened by these flows that they try to prevent refugees from crossing into their territory or they may force refugees to repatriate (Rogers and Copeland, 1993). Thus it has become more difficult to cross a border and become an official refugee; the number of internally displaced persons (IDPs) has increased at least partly due to policies such as these (see Figure 1-1).

In addition, legal barriers to refugee flows have increased, mainly in the form of restrictions on immigration and citizenship (Kushner and Knox, 1999). The increase in the number of IDPs makes the job of international organizations and nongovernmental organizations (NGOs) more difficult, since IDPs are often outside of their reach and governments and other factions may create obstacles to humanitarian intervention (Newland, 1999; Cohen, 1998). Therefore NGOs must be even more innovative in their efforts to protect and assist these groups and lower morbidity and mortality.

As noted, the human rights movement is one force that has been chipping away at the notion of sovereignty. Although the United Nations continues to uphold sovereignty in most instances, the human rights movement, along with other social, economic, and political interests, has pushed the world community to act in ways that violate the traditional notion of sovereignty in recent years: Iraq in 1991, Somalia in 1992, and Bosnia in 1992-96 (Jean, 1993). This increase in the use of collective action for the enforcement of human rights still retains a political nature, however, and is not applied universally and impartially. Instead of the East-West conflict of the Cold War era, interventions increasingly appear to have a North-South dynamic, with Northern developed countries intervening into regional and internal conflicts in the broadly-defined "South" (Rogers and Copeland, 1993).

The increase in collective action also raises the potential for greater collaboration between human rights groups, the military, and NGOs. It forces organizations like the International Committee for the Red Cross, humanitarian NGOs, and even UN agencies to reevaluate their position and often work in areas that are not safe or well protected by the military of a sovereign state or acting under the mandate of accepted international law. This has made the NGOs' job of assistance and protection even more dangerous and difficult and in turn can lead to increases in mortality among refugees and relief workers.

Sometimes, however, the changing political context can mean that NGOs have "unprecedented access" to refugees and IDPs. When governments are weak and therefore unable to limit access to populations within their borders, then major powers or coalitions of states are able to intervene rather easily. And because of their presence, ability, and resources, NGOs are the natural choice for humanitarian intervention (Stein, 2000).

In this context, the United Nations High Commissioner for Refugees, Sadako Ogata, perhaps ought to be singled out for using her office to call attention to IDPs. While certainly not alone in identifying IDPs as requiring international attention, her efforts lent authority and legitimacy to this issue, requiring at least an acknowledgement by states of this issue and its importance.

A Changing Epidemiological Context

Complex emergencies have generally been operationally defined as situations of war or civil strife, food insecurity, and/or population displacement that result in an excess mortality rate of more than 1 death per 10,000 population per day. However, many new emergencies, such as Bosnia and Kosovo, which are occurring in more developed regions of the world, do not fit this definition. The epidemiological context in developed countries is different from traditional refugee settings, such as sub-Saharan Africa and Southeast Asia. The populations are generally healthier and better nourished. Often chronic diseases, rather than communicable diseases, are an important part of the morbidity profile in developed countries. This is one reason why it is important to think about including measures of morbidity as well as mortality when assessing new emergencies (Waldman and Martone, 1999).

Health conditions are also changing; no longer are malnutrition and communicable diseases always the most pervasive threat during an emergency. Although these continue to have major impacts in many complex emergencies, physical trauma, psychosocial problems, and chronic illnesses are new issues that need attention. Measuring only mortality during an emergency says nothing about sequelae of a complex emergency that may have profound effects on the population. The psychosocial effects of trauma and disability resulting from injuries suffered during the emergency are two examples of indicators that may signify a severe emergency, even if mortality was low. For example, mortality levels in the Bosnian and Kosovar cases were lower than generally experienced in emergencies in developing countries (Waldman and Martone, 1999). Yet judgments about the severity of emergencies based on the single criterion of the number of deaths miss the suffering and human tragedy of facts like the tactical use of rape as a weapon of war, or, as in Sierra Leone, the practice of intentional mutilation that did not always result in death.

In some of today's complex emergencies, morbidity may be a better indicator of population health than mortality, because it may be easier to react to a broad range of issues as they appear, including health problems that may not be directly related to mortality, such as psychosocial issues. Measuring morbidity might also help to change the general assumption among some relief workers that their objectives are basic subsistence, followed by mortality reduction, without any other goals. Although basic needs and mortality reduction should be addressed, in some cases, morbidity may be an important indicator (Waldman and Martone, 1999). Such a change, however, carries the danger of overlooking the fact that mortality rates are tragically higher in developing country complex emergencies compared to those in developed countries. Discounting mortality rates could be used as a rationale for disproportionate expenditures in developed country crises. The ethical and policy implications are not simply solved, but need further reflection and serious discussion.

There is already a growing appreciation among the assistance and medical communities of the importance of morbidity in addition to mortality as a measure of severity and progress in emergency situations. Aid workers are now beginning to focus on care and counseling to war victims, particularly those who have been victims of rape. In addition, the issue of reproductive health has received increased attention. Finally, the experiences of refugees in the Balkans have introduced greater sensitivity to the issue of chronic illness among refugees and the problems of responding to the chronically ill in a complex emergency. This expanded mission is based on not only preventing mortality, but also "protecting life with dignity" (Waldman and Martone, 1999:1484).

New Actors and New Roles for Older Actors

Another recent development is the emergence of new actors and the creation of new roles for those responding to refugee flows and complex emergencies. The United Nations has emerged as an important actor in initiatives involving military assets in the 1990s (after years of general inactivity during the Cold War). Interventions in Angola, El Salvador, Cambodia, Bosnia, Somalia, Iraq, and Indonesia have demonstrated that the UN is now not only focusing on traditional peacekeeping, but also on "the restoration of law and order and the protection of humanitarian aid operations" (Jean, 1993; Newland, 1999). This means that the UN is intrinsically involved in protecting NGOs, and often in a de facto position of non-neutrality. Therefore, the very presence of the UN can draw severe criticism and even fire from opposing groups.

Other new roles include the presence of the military in the delivery of humanitarian assistance and a greater role for external military forces in peacekeeping, refugee protection, and operations under an international authority. The logistical capacity of many military units is unparalleled. This was recognized most notably in the case of Kurdish refugees fleeing from northern Iraq in 1991 (Centers for Disease Control and Prevention, 1991). In other situations, the ability to deliver materials efficiently and rapidly has meant that the military was called on to deliver assistance, despite the typically high cost of the military. Furthermore, there is increasing interaction between military and civilian aid workers in situations where each has more or less different roles but some overlap and a need to coordinate. Coordination is required between military and both the NGOs and international (multilateral) organizations (IOs), such as the UN High Commissioner for Refugees.

Coordination between NGOs and IOs has been and continues to be a nettlesome issue. Recently, in places like Bosnia, the multiplication of NGOs and their impact on the local economy and labor force (especially the professional labor force) has raised deep concerns. It is often the case that aid workers from more developed countries flood the local labor market and local specialists are not used to their full potential. This may mean that relief is more costly than it needs to be and also violates the current development paradigm of building local capacity.

In other cases, the targeting of aid workers by military or paramilitary groups raises the need for protection for NGOs in many locations. Guerrilla movements and their increasingly dangerous tactics—often including a lack of respect for human rights, humanitarian principles, and the Red Cross and NGOs—have made it impossible for NGOs to operate on their own without protection (Jean, 1993). This makes it even more difficult to provide high-quality relief aid. In this new era of "disengagement and privatization" by the world's governments, NGOs are encountering new responsibilities and risks. They must take control of emergency situations, because they are often the only organizations who are on the ground, but they are apt to be ill-equipped to contend with a dangerous conflict setting (Stein, 2000).

Finally, situations in which a choice must be made between two goods (or evils) requires some sort of coordinated response. For example, in the Rwandan case, Hutu forces controlled camps in Zaire, which raised the possibility that assistance might go to military forces who had committed genocide, controlled the camps, and planned an armed return to Rwanda. However, withholding aid meant that civilians in camps controlled by the military forces would suffer and perhaps die. The question of whether to give or withhold aid was a difficult one, compounded by the fact that there were many different NGOs assisting in this area (Goma Epidemiology Group, 1995).

While issues like these have no simple answer, often there is greater need of field coordination and coordinated response. If there are difficulties in coordination, it can have devastating consequences for refugees and IDPs, and even for aid workers themselves.

Increasing Attention to the Quality of Relief

Another change in the context of complex emergencies has to do with setting standards for assistance and protection. International organizations and NGOs have been working to create and implement regulations for relief aid, especially under the Sphere Project.[8] Many NGOs have joined this project, which focuses on setting minimum standards for aid, training workers to implement these standards, evaluating assistance programs, and creating accountability. These new trends are helping to ensure that the level and quality of assistance provided in emergency settings is monitored (International Federation of the Red Cross and Red Crescent Societies, 1998). And standards are critical in continued work to reduce morbidity and mortality in crisis settings.

These steps are crucial in the new climate of reduced foreign aid funding. Emergency aid is still high—almost three times its 1990 level—but within a context of an overall decrease in development aid, crises continue to flourish (International Federation of the Red Cross and Red Crescent Societies, 1998). Furthermore, NGOs are under continuous pressure to prove that their funds are being put to work in an efficient and effective manner to save lives.

A Growing Appreciation of Information Needs

The need for further research and information on complex emergencies is now becoming quite clear to many NGOs, international agencies, states, donors, and scholars. Several universities around the world have established centers for research and training on how to deal with crisis situations. NGOs are forming partnerships with these centers to create standards, evaluate their own work, and learn new ways to implement relief efforts more effectively.

Much is already known about mortality in complex emergencies, but that knowledge is not complete. Much remains unknown about complex emergencies and issues surrounding appropriate responses, including ethical issues, management of specific diseases, and understanding how to treat specific populations. Reproductive health and mental health are

---

[8] "The Sphere Project was launched by a group of humanitarian agencies . . . to develop a set of universal minimum standards in core areas of humanitarian assistance. The aim of the Project is to improve the quality of assistance provided to people affected by disasters and to enhance the accountability of the humanitarian system in disaster response" (Sphere Project, 2000).

two of the most important areas in need of further study (Waldman and Martone, 1999). In order to improve understanding, response, and assistance to forced migrants, research and collaboration must continue. The case studies in this volume are an example of a step towards more and better knowledge of mortality in complex emergencies.

DATA ISSUES

While the international assistance community is confident about the general course of responses to complex emergencies to reduce mortality and is beginning to understand the new contexts for complex emergencies, much more still needs to be known about mortality levels and trends and measurement of them. Why is it important to focus on collecting good mortality data in emergencies? Approximate data are generally sufficient for preliminary assessment of a crisis situation and for mobilizing public support and resources. However, as situations develop, the need for more precise data increases. Relief workers must be able to better estimate the population's needs and evaluate their own performance to ensure the best quality relief and the least morbidity and mortality (Reed et al., 1998). Nevertheless, excess mortality data are often the result of crude attempts to obtain approximate estimates. In addition to the generally difficult conditions for data collection in ongoing emergencies, there are a number of other issues that hinder the development of more reliable, comparative data on mortality that would improve the analysis and understanding of trends in demographic processes among forced migrants caught in complex emergencies. As Figure 1-9 (in the Appendix) and the appendix illustrate, even after crises end there is continued uncertainty about the total excess mortality during the crises.

Uniform Protocols for Data Collection

Relief workers, particularly medical personnel, seek the baseline information needed to respond to the most pressing health problems and develop monitoring systems. However, in the chaotic situation of a complex emergency, these systems are often poorly coordinated and sometimes even duplicate information. Many times, there is no general agreement or protocol on what data to collect or the appropriate methods to follow to ensure quality, interpretation, and comparability in order to assess the severity of problems and to provide markers for assessing progress over time. Field personnel need better systems of data collection to generate the information they need to plan, even in rudimentary ways, their response to the specific problems of a complex emergency. It is not that data collection as it is currently done is without merit. Much knowledge of mortality in complex emergencies results from such data collection by the medical community. However, questions of quality and comparability retard efforts to accumulate a body of knowledge that would facilitate sophisticated analysis of the determinants and pace of mortality change under stressful situations.

Denominators

The estimation of a population at risk in the construction of any demographic rate seems deceptively simple, but unfortunately it is often wrong and/or the result of compromise. In emergency situations, the basic estimation of the total number of refugees, which is needed to construct even a crude mortality rate, is elusive. The difficult conditions of emergency situations can make producing even rudimentary estimates an extreme challenge (see appendix). In addition, there are several specific reasons for population overestimation in crises. The leaders of displaced persons may try to hide those who are not legitimate refugees (those who have been involved in war crimes or military operations) in with the rest of the displaced population and thus inflate the numbers. Refugees may also try to register themselves more than once in order to gain more food rations. Out-migrations and deaths may also be underreported for the same reasons. When refugees are located within a host country community, local residents may register as refugees in order to obtain food and medical aid. Finally, refugee events are quite fluid and change rapidly.

On the other hand, refugee and displaced populations may be underestimated for a variety of reasons. Refugees who are self-settled among local populations may be difficult to count because they are hidden or continue to be on the move. If relief workers are not permitted access to the populations, then they are likely to misestimate their numbers. Those who are sick, impoverished, or malnourished may be hidden or cut off from the rest of the group and therefore not counted.

Thus, estimates of the same events taken from different sources often vary greatly. Perhaps the most familiar example of this is the different population estimates of the Rwandan refugees in Goma, Zaire, in 1994. Estimates from different agencies and NGOs ranged from 500,000 to 800,000, making it impossible to determine the mortality rate with any accuracy (Goma Epidemiology Group, 1995). In many situations, therefore, even if there is confidence in the estimated number of deaths, it is not a foregone conclusion that one can estimate the mortality rate with any confidence in the result (see also the case studies on Afghanistan and North Korea in the appendix).

Composition of Denominators

Even more demanding than estimating the total population is obtaining information on the composition of a given population. Of special interest in the study of mortality is age composition because of the vulnerability of children less than five years of age in developing countries. This age group is vulnerable even under normal circumstances, but much more so in situations of conflict, violence, and displacement (Davis, 1996). The age composition of a refugee population can have very important effects on the crude mortality rate. A population with a higher proportion of young children and elderly (like many developing country populations) will probably have a higher crude mortality rate than a population with a middle-aged distribution, because children under five years of age will probably experience higher mortality rates. Whether mortality is "excess" or not and why mortality is "elevated" are both a function of a population's age composition. This is a problem in many emergencies because only crude mortality rates are collected and therefore nothing is known about age- and sex-specific mortality rates. Even when age-specific mortality rates are known, they are generally only broken down into two categories: children under five years of age and others, which does not permit careful analysis.

Thus, age composition may explain some "excess" mortality. However, as noted above, if large proportions of children under the age of five, who may be over-represented in the refugee population, die in the early stages of a complex emergency, then the converse of excess mortality may occur. It is possible that the remaining population might appear to have lower than normal mortality because of the age composition of the surviving population. Heavy loss of vulnerable populations in an acute phase of an emergency, followed by the availability of assistance (including some assistance elements, such as vaccinations, that may not normally be available), may result in mortality levels for survivors that are significantly lower than those in the pre-emergency situation. There are various scenarios about the effects of early deaths on different groups within various populations that may affect subsequent mortality patterns. What is lacking is systematic data on these situations and analysis of mortality patterns within different populations.

In short, mortality rates in all emergencies should be standardized for age and sex, which requires some ability to decompose the population by these characteristics. If this is not done, then reliance on crude mortality rates as the major indicator of the severity of a complex emergency can lead to incorrect conclusions.

Collecting Mortality Data

There are many ways to collect mortality data in refugee settings, including burial site surveillance, collecting information from hospital and burial records, community-based reporting systems, and population surveys. However, none of these methods is flawless. Some of the reasons why data may be inaccurate are:

- Poorly representative population sample surveys;
- Failure of families to report all deaths for fear of losing food ration entitlements;
- Inaccurate estimates of affected populations for the purpose of calculating mortality rates; and
- Lack of standard reporting procedures (Toole and Waldman, 1997: 287).

Mortality rates are often underestimated because of deaths being undercounted and populations being overestimated. Secure and well-organized refugee camps seem to have generally produced the best estimates, while it is very difficult to get good mortality data on scattered populations and internally displaced persons. Mortality may be skewed in one direction or another because those with the highest risk of death are drawn to camps where there is food and medical attention or because those with the highest risk of death are in areas with the least access to the relief aid (Toole and Waldman, 1997). It is very difficult to compare mortality survey results from different settings because of the huge variation in methods. In Somalia between 1991 and 1993, 23 field surveys were found to have extreme differences in populations, sampling methods, units of analysis, computation of rates, and analysis techniques (Boss et al., 1994). However, it is hoped that efforts like the Sphere Project will increase the comparability between data from different settings.

Sampling

Sampling is the process whereby researchers determine a subset of the population under study from which to collect data that will hopefully be representative of the entire population. If the sample is properly drawn, then one should be able to make inferences about a population based on the characteristics of a sample. Although sampling is already a challenging enterprise under normal circumstances, in complex emergencies and refugee settings, it becomes even more difficult. In addition to "normal" issues that may bias the sample, because the total population is often unknown and unreachable, it is very difficult to obtain a representative and unbiased sample in an emergency setting.

Again, the major bias of current knowledge of demographic processes among refugee and internally displaced populations is the heavy reliance on information gathered from populations in camps. This is because of the relative ease of sampling and collecting data in a camp setting, where the sampling frame, or total population, is known, or area samples of a confined population are used. However, some scholars have argued that over 60 percent of Africa's refugees do not reside in camps; they live among the population in host countries (Harrell-Bond, 1994; Van Damme, 1995). What is known about refugee mortality may not hold true for non-camp populations. The reality is that the potential differences between these two populations are unknown because most information comes from camp situations where refugees are collectively aided by relief and protection agencies.

Furthermore, because estimates of the total size of a refugee population are so difficult to obtain, any attempts to sample from this more or less unknown universe become problematic. Sampling can move from a concern with population parameters to sampling geographically or spatially. In camp settings, such approaches have been implemented by dividing space into coordinated blocks and collecting data within specific blocks or sampling areas (Médecins Sans Frontières, 1997). In non-camp settings, such techniques are less useful unless one has knowledge of the spatial distribution of refugees among the host population. Therefore, other nonrandom sampling methods, such as snowball sampling, where one finds one refugee who then identifies other refugees to be included in the sample, must be used. However, these types of sampling techniques often mean that some refugees and demographic events, like deaths, may be missed.

Recall

The effect of the experience of a complex emergency on people's ability to recall events, and whether it is more of an issue than in normal situations, is unknown. Depending on specific cultural beliefs about death, psychosocial trauma, and other issues, it may be quite difficult to get an accurate estimate of mortality based on a population survey in an emergency setting. The impact of recall on monitoring and surveillance is not trivial because it is important in trying to develop baseline parameters.

Issues of data quality, interpretation, and methodology are not limited to those mentioned above. These are examples of issues that come up again and again in discussions of mortality patterns in complex emergencies. In many published papers, there is only a brief allusion in the form of a caveat for interpretation of data. Progress in understanding levels, trends, patterns, determinants, and consequences of mortality in complex emergencies requires attention to these technical issues from demographers, epidemiologists, and statisticians. Although the issues may seem sterile and esoteric, they have a large impact on what is known and consequently how relief workers are likely to respond to crisis situations.

OVERVIEW OF THE VOLUME

This introduction covers a broad amount of territory about information on mortality in complex emergencies and related data issues. It provides a basic overview of the state of knowledge, the gaps that need attention, and aspects of the social and operational situation that affect data collection, interpretation, and application. The case studies in this volume look at the specific examples of Rwanda, Kosovo, North Korea, and Cambodia. These case studies are drawn from four different regions and examine four different types of crises. They try to provide a best estimate of what we know but also illustrate concretely the issues reviewed above and the need for progress in the knowledge base used to address complex emergencies.

In the first case study, Dominique Legros, Christopher Paquet, and Pierre Nabeth describe the flight of Rwandan refugees into the forests of Eastern Zaire (now the Democratic Republic of the Congo) and discuss mortality at various stages of the forced migration that occurred following the 1994 genocide. Using a combination of surveillance systems and retrospective mortality surveys, they estimate mortality rates for the same refugee population at four different points in time and in four different geographic locations. The pattern that emerges is quite disturbing; by the final estimation, only about 20 percent of the original refugee population remained and the rest were either dead or missing. The authors also discuss the merits and drawbacks of both mortality estimation methods.

Brent Burkholder, Paul Spiegel, and Peter Salama examine these same methods—surveillance and retrospective surveys—in an entirely different population: Albanian Kosovar refugees in March to June 1999. One set of data was collected from surveillance systems that were operational in refuge areas in Albania and the Former Yugoslav Republic of Macedonia (FYROM) during the refugee crisis. The second data set was collected in Kosovo in September 1999, after the majority of the refugees had returned home. The authors compare and contrast the results of these two efforts and find that overall mortality in the Kosovo crisis was relatively low. The different nature of the populations and the crisis in a more developed region raises several methodological issues about estimating mortality, such as the importance of chronic diseases, reproductive health, and psychosocial trauma.

In the third case study, Court Robinson, Myung Lee, Ken Hill, and Gilbert Burnham use indirect estimation techniques to estimate mortality rates among an isolated population suffering from famine: North Korea. By interviewing North Korean migrants who crossed the border into China in search of food about their own household experiences and the experiences of a sibling, nonmigrant household, they were able to estimate mortality rates. Although the sample is not representative, the study gives insight into what is happening inside North Korea.

The final case was not originally presented at the workshop, but commissioned afterwards. Patrick Heuveline describes a variety of data sources and techniques that can be used to estimate the total excess mortality during the Cambodian crisis of 1975 to 1979. Survey and census data are discussed, but ultimately the focus is again on indirect estimation techniques, including demographic projection methods to attempt to estimate total excess mortality and decomposition methods to get at age- and cause-specific mortality.

Finally, in his reflections on the four case studies, Manuel Carballo ponders the difficulty and necessity of collecting statistics in emergency situations. He reminds practitioners and researchers alike that each crisis is a unique event and must be understood not only on the basis of its similarities to other events, but on the basis of its specificity.

NEXT STEPS

What are some potential topics for future research on these issues? There are many issues that researchers and practitioners should examine as they continue to work on understanding mortality patterns in complex emergencies:

- Increase and improve the collection of data by age, sex, and other characteristics in complex emergencies to enhance our understanding of mortality patterns for population subgroups;
- Examine mortality patterns by age group and compare these patterns to those of populations that are not in crisis;
- Improve techniques for the evaluation of humanitarian interventions by NGOs and other aid organizations;
- Improve our understanding of the long-term consequences of complex emergencies on morbidity and mortality, including psychosocial and reproductive health; and
- Document, compare and validate methods for rapid assessment techniques in emergencies.

These are only a few of the potential research and data needs for learning more about mortality in complex emergencies. The volume signifies an increased appreciation of the need for data and the shallowness of the knowledge base about demographic processes among displaced populations. In addition to continued research on mortality, topics such as information on reproductive health and fertility and mental illness are beginning to be studied in forced migrant populations. Perhaps with a new appreciation of the utility of this information, more attention will be given to improving the quality of research on refugees and IDPs. With improved data and analysis, policies and programs can be created and adjusted accordingly to best assist forced migrants in each situation.

REFERENCES

Abiri, E.
  2000   The securitisation of migration. Unpublished Ph.D. dissertation, Department of Peace and Development Research, Gothenburg University.
Boss, L.P., M.J. Toole, and R. Yip
  1994   Assessments of mortality, morbidity, and nutritional status in Somalia during the 1991-1992 famine. *Journal of the American Medical Association* 272:371-376.
Centers for Disease Control and Prevention
  1990   Update: Health and nutritional profiles of refugees—Ethiopia, 1989-1990. *Morbidity and Mortality Weekly Report* 39:707-709, 715-718.
  1991   Public health consequences of acute displacement of Iraqi citizens, March-May 1991. *Morbidity and Mortality Weekly Report* 40(26):443-446.
  1992   Famine-affected, refugee, and displaced populations: Recommendations for public health issues. *Morbidity and Mortality Weekly Report* 41:RR-13.
  1993a   Mortality among newly arrived Mozambican refugees: Zimbabwe and Malawi, 1992. *Morbidity and Mortality Weekly Report* 42:468-469, 475-477.
  1993b   Status of public health: Bosnia and Herzegovina, August-September 1993. *Morbidity and Mortality Weekly Report* 42:973, 979-982.
Coale, A.J., P. Demeny, and B. Vaughan
  1983   *Regional Model Life Tables and Stable Populations,* 2nd edition. San Diego, CA: Academic Press, Inc.
Cohen, R.
  1998   Recent trends in protection and assistance for IDPs. Pp. 3-9 in J. Hampton, ed., *Internally Displaced People: A Global Survey.* London: Earthscan Publications, Global IDP Survey, and Norwegian Refugee Council.
Davis, A.P.
  1996   Targeting the vulnerable in emergency situations: Who is vulnerable? *Lancet* 348:868-871.
Elias, C.J., B.H. Alexander, and T. Sokly
  1990   Infectious disease control in a long-term refugee camp: The role of epidemiologic surveillance and investigation. *American Journal of Public Health* 80(7):824-828.
Goma Epidemiology Group
  1995   Public health impact of Rwandan refugee crisis. What happened in Goma, Zaire, in July 1994? *Lancet* 345:339-344.

Hansch, S.
    1999   *The Evolution of Mortality Patterns in Complex Emergencies.* Unpublished paper presented at Workshop on Mortality Patterns in Complex Emergencies, National Academy of Sciences, November 19, 1999, Washington, D.C.
Harrell-Bond, B.
    1994   Pitch the tents. *The New Republic* September 19-26.
International Federation of the Red Cross and Red Crescent Societies
    1998   *World Disasters Report 1998.* Oxford, UK: Oxford University Press.
Jean, F., ed.
    1993   *Life, Death, and Aid: The Médecins Sans Frontières Report on World Crisis Intervention.* London and New York: Routledge.
Kushner, T., and K. Knox
    1999   *Refugees in an Age of Genocide: Global, National, and Local Perspectives during the Twentieth Century.* London: Frank Cass.
Médecins Sans Frontières
    1997   *Refugee Health: An Approach to Emergency Situations.* London: Macmillan.
Moore, P.S., A.A. Marfin, L.E. Quenemoen, B.D. Gessner, and Y.S. Ayub
    1993   Mortality rates in displaced and resident populations of Central Somalia during the famine of 1992. *Lancet* 341:935-938.
Natsios, A.S.
    1997   *U.S. Foreign Policy and the Four Horsemen of the Apocalypse: Humanitarian Relief in Complex Emergencies.* Westport, CT: Praeger Publishers and the Center for Strategic and International Studies.
Newland, K.
    1999   The decade in review. Pp. 14-21 in *World Refugee Survey 1999.* Washington, D.C.: Immigration and Refugee Services of America.
Noji, E.K., ed.
    1997   *The Public Health Consequences of Disasters.* New York: Oxford University Press.
Person-Karell, B.
    1989   The relationship between child malnutrition and crude mortality among 42 refugee populations. Unpublished master's thesis. Atlanta, GA: Emory University.
Population Reference Bureau
    2000   *World Population Data Sheet.* Washington, DC: Population Reference Bureau.
Reed, H., J. Haaga, and C. Keely, eds.
    1998   *The Demography of Forced Migration: Summary of a Workshop.* Washington, DC: National Academy Press.
Rogers, R., and E. Copeland
    1993   *Forced Migration: Policy Issues in the Post-Cold War World.* Medford, MA: Tufts University.
Shryock, H.S., J.S. Siegel, and associates
    1976   *The Methods and Materials of Demography.* Condensed edition by Edward G. Stockwell. San Diego, CA: Academic Press.
Sphere Project
    2000   *Humanitarian Charter and Minimum Standards in Disaster Response.* [Online]. Available: http://www.sphereproject.org [December 19, 2000].
Stein, J.G.
    2000   New challenges to conflict resolution: Humanitarian nongovernmental organizations in complex emergencies. Pp. 383-419 in *International Conflict Resolution After the Cold War.* Committee on International Conflict Resolution, Paul C. Stern and Daniel Druckman, eds. Washington, DC: National Academy Press.

Toole, M.J., and R. Bhatia
    1992   A case study of Somali refugees in Hartisheik A camp, eastern Ethiopia: Health and nutrition profile, July 1988-June 1989. *Journal of Refugee Studies* 5:313-326.
Toole, M.J., S. Galson, and W. Brady
    1993   Are war and public health compatible? *Lancet* 341:935-938.
Toole, M.J., R.J. Steketee, R.J. Waldman, and P. Nieburg
    1989   Measles prevention and control in emergency settings. *Bulletin of the World Health Organization* 67:381-388.
Toole, M.J., and R.J. Waldman
    1988   An analysis of mortality trends among refugee populations in Somalia, Sudan, and Thailand. *Bulletin of the World Health Organization* 66(2):237-247.
    1990   Prevention of excess mortality in refugee and displaced populations in developing countries. *Journal of the American Medical Association* 263:3296-3302.
    1997   The public health aspects of complex emergencies and refugee situations. *Annual Review of Public Health* 18:283-312.
United Nations High Commissioner for Refugees
    2000   *Refugees and Others of Concern to UNHCR: 1999 Statistical Overview.* Geneva: Registration and Statistical Unit, Programme Coordination Section, United Nations High Commissioner for Refugees.
United States Committee for Refugees
    2000   *World Refugee Survey 2000.* Washington, DC: Immigration and Refugee Services of America.
Van Damme, W.
    1995   Do refugees belong in camps? Experiences from Goma and Guinea. *Lancet* 346:360-362.
Wæver, O., B. Buzan, M. Kelstrup, and P. Lemaitre
    1993   *Identity, Migration, and the New Security Agenda in Europe.* New York: St. Martin's Press.
Waldman, R., and G. Martone
    1999   Public health and complex emergencies: New issues, new conditions. *American Journal of Public Health* 89(10):1483-1485.
Watson, F., I. Kulenovic, and J. Vespa
    1995   Nutritional status and food security: Winter nutrition monitoring in Sarajevo, 1993-1994. *European Journal of Clinical Nutrition* 49:S23-S32.
World Bank
    1991   *World Development Report 1991: The Challenge of Development.* New York: Oxford University Press.
    1992   *World Development Report 1992: Development and the Environment.* New York: Oxford University Press.
    1994   *World Development Report 1994: Infrastructure for Development.* New York: Oxford University Press.
    1995   *World Development Report 1995: Workers in an Integrating World.* New York: Oxford University Press.
    1996   *World Development Report 1996: From Plan to Market.* New York: Oxford University Press.

APPENDIX: FIVE ILLUSTRATIONS OF UNCERTAINTY: MORTALITY IN AFGHANISTAN, BOSNIA, NORTH KOREA, RWANDA, AND SIERRA LEONE

Steven Hansch

This appendix presents short narratives of five countries that have experienced recent conflict, in which data on mortality are difficult to ascertain. They are included as a kind of rough overview on how general estimates of mortality are generated in emergencies, rather than a scientific study of mortality estimation in these settings. This is done in order to give readers a sense of the real difficulties of data collection and analyzing the many different estimates that are produced in situations involving conflict and forced migration. Five cases are presented:

- Afghanistan in the 1980s and 1990s,
- Bosnia-Herzegovina during the period of civil conflict, 1992-1995,
- North Korea during its famine crisis of 1995-1998,
- Rwanda during the year of genocide in 1994, and
- Sierra Leone from 1992 to 1998.

In each case, evidence is culled from a variety of sources, including interviews, published literature, news wires, and firsthand observations. In many cases, the data provide only indirect, circumstantial, or limited views of the mortality pattern, and at times the data were drawn from points in time outside the periods of interest. Each case begins with a brief discussion of the situation, followed by evidence for and conclusions about the estimates of excess mortality. Finally, there is a review of mortality risk factors in each setting. Figure 1-9 shows the range of estimates of excess mortality for each of these five complex emergencies.

AFGHANISTAN

Afghanistan has suffered cyclical conflict, displacement, massacres, food insecurity, epidemics, collapsed health services, and earthquakes since the 1970s. During this period, virtually no international aid organizations have been able to observe conditions in much of the country, although groups like International Medical Corps (IMC), CARE, and Save the Children have had periodic access to Kabul and the eastern districts. Afghanistan's reported population of 24.8 million is therefore very difficult to confirm, and in any case, millions of Afghan citizens continue to

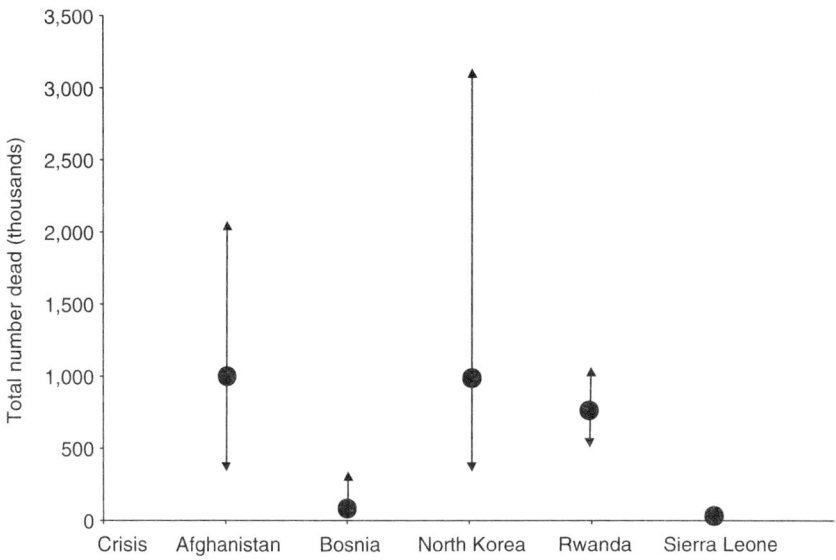

FIGURE 1–9   Range of mortality estimates in five complex humanitarian emergencies.

live in Iran or in refugee camps in Pakistan, where many of them fled during the conflict with the Soviet Union that began in 1979.

Evidence of Mortality

Inside Afghanistan

The war in Kabul in 1993 reportedly led to 23,000 deaths, and fighting in the north during the mid- and late 1990s led to numerous massacres and disappearances. Indiscriminate shelling during 1994 and the first three months of 1995 killed 13,000 people, injured 50,000, and left the city without water or electricity (Cohen, 1996). In 1993, Médecins Sans Frontières (MSF) conducted a retrospective, population-based, household survey of 600 families in Kabul and found a crude mortality rate between 0.5 and 1.0. Mortality was highest among those who had lived in Kabul for a long time and was usually due to gunshot wound. For children, however, deaths were due to measles, diarrhea, and acute respiratory tract infections (Gessner, 1994).

Refugee Camps in Pakistan

Media coverage during the conflict with the Soviet Union characterized the refugees as poor, desperate, hungry, and ill. Due to political
stakes and the media coverage, most Westerners believed that the refugees were living in terrible conditions.

Upon review, however, there was never any substantial excess mortality in the camps. One relief coordinator for Oxfam (a nongovernmental
organization) reported that "The refugee camps themselves were relatively free of any of the problems inside Afghanistan itself. Also, as time
went on, Afghans in the North-West Frontier Province began quite rapidly to find employment; there was very little evidence of malnutrition in
the camps" (Bennett, 1999). In some camps, however, child mortality
was high, particularly in the southern refugee camps, in Queta Province,
due to the failure to immunize the children (Boss et al., 1986).

Estimates of Excess Mortality

The last 20 or more years have been a period of political and social
disintegration characterized by ongoing mass migration, arms trade, and
rule of law at gunpoint. An entire generation has grown up in Afghanistan knowing nothing but conflict; there is no clear baseline mortality rate
and no discrete event or disaster period to contrast to other periods. Many
sources refer to relatively high numbers of casualties (Sliwinski, 1988;
Khalidi, 1991). Wallensteen and Sollenberg (1998) report yearly estimates
of casualty figures in the annual surveys of conflict. But total excess
mortality is unknown; it could lie anywhere between 200,000 and 2 million.

Mortality Risk Factors

Mortality risk factors in Afghanistan include landmines, communicable diseases, food insecurity, and natural disasters.

Afghanistan is one of the more heavily mined countries in the world,
with ongoing risk from one landmine per person and over 10,000
landmine victims (Lindenberg, 1999). In some areas, it is likely that a high
proportion of deaths is attributable to landmines. However, most
landmine injury surveillance comes from hospital reporting, which underestimates those persons killed immediately by the blast (McDiarmid,
1995; Andersson et al., 1995; Coupland, 1991). Landmine injuries tend to
affect men more than women, and adolescents and young adults more
than other age groups.

Communicable diseases account for most of the excess mortality in areas outside of immediate combat zones. Among children seen in a Kabul hospital, half of all deaths were related to diarrhea, and two-thirds of all patients seen were malnourished (Choudhry et al., 1989). A recent report from Jalalabad finds that roughly half of hospital cases are related in one way or another to either malaria or typhoid (Pilsczek, 1996).

In 1987, the main concern of humanitarian aid agencies in Afghanistan was food security, especially given large projected returns of refugees to central and southern provinces. However, there are very few data on food insecurity inside Afghanistan.

In addition to these other factors, Afghanistan has high excess mortality due to natural disasters. One of two earthquakes that occurred in 1998 resulted in 5,000 deaths (Ivker, 1990; International Federation of the Red Cross and Red Crescent Societies, 1999).

BOSNIA-HERZEGOVINA

In spring 1992, Serbian forces attacked Sarajevo, and thus began a war for Bosnia-Herzegovina, which had a population of approximately 4.5 million. During the war, roughly 3 million people became refugees; estimates of internally displaced persons inside Bosnia were around 1.2 million. The Serbs laid siege to Sarajevo, cut it off from outside contact, and began bombing and sniping at civilians in 1993.

Evidence of Mortality

Some sample surveys have shown episodes of high mortality from various causes, mostly killing: a survey by MSF-Netherlands in April 1993 found a crude mortality rate of 2.3. The event causing the largest excess mortality of the Bosnia crisis took place in Srebrenica in 1995, when an estimated 7,300 to 8,000 men (out of an overall civilian population of 40,000) were captured, disappeared, and murdered. While the event itself was widely discussed, the true number of missing men has not been precisely estimated. These deaths were not combat-related: they were executions, for which the principal risk factor was being an adult Muslim male resident of the city.

The International Committee for the Red Cross (ICRC) established a database of persons reported missing to help disrupted families. Of the 20,000 persons on the list, several hundred have been found, but it is widely believed that most of the 20,000 who remain missing are dead. The Bosnia State Commission on Missing Persons estimates that 28,000 are missing.

Forensics research has been extremely valuable in reconstructing patterns of adult mortality in Bosnia. Between 1995 and 1998, approximately

400 mass graves were identified, each holding between 3 and 300 dead bodies. Various groups working on exhumations are collaborating with the efforts to trace missing persons, including Physicians for Human Rights, a U.S. nongovernmental organization (NGO), and the International Crimes Tribunal for Yugoslavia (ICTY). It is difficult to estimate the true number of mass graves, but there is reason to believe that there may be as many as 600.

Estimates of Excess Mortality

Total excess mortality from diseases, urban massacres, disappearances, and battles adds up to about 60,000 to 80,000 deaths, yet estimates of 150,000 to 200,000 deaths have been given credence by some policy makers (Médecins Sans Frontières, 1995). These high estimates are based on the assumption that non-Muslim deaths totaled no more than 10,000, which may be a questionable premise.

The high-end estimate of 200,000 originates from the Bosnian government itself and was taken up by other groups, such as the United Nations High Commissioner for Refugees (UNHCR), in order to draw world attention to Bosnia. In late 1993, the United Nations estimated that some 230,000 persons were either dead or missing (Minear et al., 1994). Some government analysts also estimated very high mortality: in November 1995, the U.S. Central Intelligence Agency estimated 156,000 civilian deaths (Borden and Caplan, 1996). George Kenney, an U.S. Department of State official involved in the Bosnia crisis, has challenged these estimates. Kenney argued that mortality was substantially lower, based on Red Cross and other international agency estimates (Kenney, 1995). NGO aid workers, the U.S. Centers for Disease Control, and the Stockholm International Peace Research Institute generally support his figure of 25,000 to 60,000. Within the U.S. Department of Defense, there is disagreement about the best estimate, but it ranges from 70,000 to 95,000, which is closer to Kenney's original 1995 estimate.

Mortality Risk Factors

The main risk factors have been exposure to battle conditions and gunshots (Centers for Disease Control and Prevention, 1993). Violent trauma accounted for 15 percent of total morbidity, 56 percent of total mortality, and affected two-thirds of the civilian population.

By and large, communicable diseases, chronic diseases, and malnutrition did not cause substantial numbers of deaths, although simply being in a hospital may have been correlated with mortality, since hospitals were bombed during intense fighting in the town of Mostar (Horton,

1999). When Serbs shelled the Gorazde hospital in April 1994, 700 were reported killed (Cohen, 1998).

The availability of field hospitals appears to make a large difference in the survival of the battle-wounded in settings like Bosnia (Maricevic and Erceg, 1997). Approximately 4,000 trauma and surgical cases were seen during the first 10 months of war in Zenica. While Bosnia had qualified surgical personnel, the limiting factors were more often lack of power supply in the hospitals, new equipment, and drugs (Pretto et al., 1994).

The main mortality risk factor in Sarajevo was going to the river to obtain water for household use, because of the danger of getting caught in sniper fire. Despite efforts by international humanitarian agencies, internally displaced persons received inadequate protection. One observer has argued that the creation of exclusion zones could have reduced mortality (Cuny, 1996:209):

> In Bosnia, the imposition of a total exclusion zone for heavy weapons around the besieged capital of Sarajevo in February 1994 had the potential for ending the war. The Serbs were ordered to either withdraw their weapons or place them in designated weapons collection points within the zone. Any heavy weapon firing inside the zone would be subject to air strikes by NATO. The imposition of the zone dramatically altered the strategic picture by denying the Serbs the ability to capture the capital. Had similar zones been placed around other Bosnian cities, the fighting might have ended.

NORTH KOREA

North Korea (the Democratic People's Republic of Korea) has been isolated since the fall of the Soviet Union and therefore very vulnerable during times of crisis. Between 1992 and 1995, government food ration distributions were drastically curtailed to citizens in the northeastern provinces. In 1995, after 23 inches of rain fell during 10 days in July and August, North Korea declared a disaster and appealed for international food aid while it repaired its damaged agriculture and infrastructure. This was an unusual shift for the government, which had previously resisted admission of need or failure. A year later, a drought hit the country, leading to an even greater need for foreign aid.

The peak of North Korea's famine appears to have been in late 1996 and early 1997, and international food aid grew during those years, peaking in 1998. It appeared to save large numbers of lives. International aid, including over a million tons of food from China, and several million tons of food from the World Food Program and the United States, permitted new observers to enter North Korea for the first time in decades.

Evidence of Mortality

Mortality estimates in North Korea are prone to many potential biases, including:

- Observational bias related to lack of access to the population by independent authorities and international aid workers;
- Observational bias related to the intrinsic invisibility of high-risk individuals: many manifestations of poverty, malnutrition and related mortality tend to be hidden;
- Observational bias related to the areas where aid workers work: this can also lead to over-reporting because of biases on the part of aid workers;
- Time-frame validity: this may be due to mis-reporting of dates by individuals or purposeful mis-reporting of dates by governments;
- Construct validity: it is difficult to define deaths due only to famine because of intervening factors;
- Reporting bias for political reasons: this may be mis-reporting by the government, by civilians, or by refugees; or
- Sampling bias because of the use of data from refugees from North Korea: refugees who have fled North Korea are more likely to be fleeing from situations in which crisis is more intense, the risk of death is higher, and, statistically, more deaths have occurred.

Estimates of Excess Mortality

Estimates of mortality due to famine in North Korea come from a number of sources. The government of South Korea recently estimated that 2 million North Koreans have died due to the crisis. The North Korean government's official estimates are that 220,000 deaths have occurred.

One recent study indicates that mortality peaked in 1997, with a crude mortality rate of 56.0 deaths per 1,000 population per year. The average rate over three years (1995 to 1997) was 43.0 (Robinson et al., 1999). This research is the strongest evidence to date of confirmed mortality in North Korea, although it represents only one geographic portion of the country. Since 20 deaths per 1,000 per year would be normal for a country like North Korea, a three-year average rate of 43 implies excess mortality of about 23 per 1,000 during this period, or net 69 deaths per 1,000 population. If this is representative of about one-third of North Korea's total population, this would translate to approximately 450,000 excess deaths.

Over the last two years, World Vision and the Korean community in the United States have publicized interviews conducted by Buddhist monks of refugees fleeing North Korea into South Korea, coming up with estimates of closer to 3 million deaths. These groups may have political motives for overestimating mortality, however.

Another key report is by former U.S. disaster coordinator Andrew Natsios (1999). Applying the mortality rates derived by Robinson et al. (1999) to the general population, he concludes that roughly 2.4 million people died. This high-end estimate is apparently based on an arbitrary extrapolation, however, and may be very unrealistic.

Mortality Risk Factors

The clearest cause of mortality in famines is wasting malnutrition, and this is certainly the case in North Korea. In 1998, the European Union, the World Food Programme (WFP), the United Nations Children's Fund (UNICEF), and Save the Children, working with UNHCR, estimated food insecurity malnutrition in North Korea. Their surveys, conducted at the end of the famine, found moderate levels of malnutrition that would not lead to high future mortality rates (16 percent moderately or severely malnourished) (European Union et al., 1998). They also suggest that death rates had not been very high until then.

According to Natsios (1999), mortality was lower among many small farmers who cultivated secret gardens, strategically pre-harvesting some grain crops for surreptitious grain stores to help their families survive. The only other groups with direct availability to crops are the military, who have become involved both in monitoring and in helping with agricultural production.

Extrapolating from similar crises in other countries, it is highly likely that excess mortality is disproportionately higher for young children, especially girls, the elderly, those working in service professions (outside the government and the military), and those living in remote areas and northern provinces.

RWANDA

After years of simmering tensions between Hutu and Tutsi ethnic groups, Rwanda erupted in the early 1990s, when civil conflict flared after Tutsi army incursions from Uganda, leading to the displacement of 900,000 people due to the 1993 fighting. In 1994, the worst genocide in recent times took place, followed by retribution killings of civilians, by excess mortality in refugee camps related to poor health, and ongoing battles with internally displaced persons inside Rwanda. The largest share of excess mortality, however, was due to the systematic campaign of ethnic cleansing by the ruling Hutu government prior to April 1994.

Evidence of Mortality

Throughout Rwanda

The killings in Rwanda took place across the country all at once, but the lines of population displacement proceeded in a wave following the progress of the Tutsi forces, who streamed southward from Uganda. Most of the deaths from the crisis occurred in a short span of 10 weeks in 1994, and most resulted from one-on-one attacks by Hutu villagers against their neighbors, most often with machetes (Prunier, 1995). ICRC and MSF estimated during the early phases of the genocide that 200,000 were killed in the first three to four weeks. The estimated number of deaths after six weeks was 500,000 (Weiss, 1999). However, these estimates are highly speculative.

In the Camps

Very high excess mortality occurred in the Rwandan refugee camps, but only briefly and only in one area: 35,000 in approximately one week in July 1994 in the camps based around Goma, due to cholera. During the first month, approximately 50,000 died in North Kivu (Goma Epidemiology Group, 1995). And 40,000 deaths were reported by the gravediggers. Later, when these same refugees were forcibly returned to Rwanda in 1996, there was another cholera outbreak affecting 10,000, with only 46 deaths (Brown et al., 1996).

The highest death rate for a defined sub-population was among refugee children who matriculated into centers of care for unaccompanied minors (who were assumed to be mostly orphans, but were at least dislocated from their families). Their mortality was up to 80 times above baseline (Dowell et al., 1995).

Estimates of Excess Mortality

The UN has estimated that 800,000 died. But the most recent report of Human Rights Watch (HRW) argues that this estimate is high because it includes non-genocide causes (Des Forges, 1999). HRW estimates range from 500,000 to 600,000 genocide-specific mortality. Africa Rights (an NGO) estimates that the genocide totaled 750,000 deaths in Rwanda, based on strong evidence of mass executions, but this estimate may be biased by the personal interest of the authors (Omaar and de Waal, 1994). When one adds in all the collateral deaths related to the complex emergency, however, the total excess mortality for the period is around 750,000.

Mortality Risk Factors

Rwanda was a very complex emergency with many mortality risks. Most of the deaths occurred in three sub-populations:

- Tutsi civilians residing in Rwanda, particularly those in the north and public officials;
- Resident Hutus who were not part of the Interhamwe (the Hutu militia group who massacred Tutsis) but were suspect of allegiance to the Forces Armées Rwandaises (FAR), the former Rwandan army, in mid-1994, when retribution killings occurred, and in 1995, when internally displaced persons were subject to intolerance; and
- Refugees in North Kivu who were subject to a combination of shigella, cholera, dehydration, and malnutrition.

SIERRA LEONE

Civil conflict began in Sierra Leone in 1991 and has been heavily influenced by spillover from the ongoing conflict in Liberia. In general, the war has pitted the democratic government against Revolutionary Unity Front (RUF) rebels, backed by Charles Taylor's militia in Liberia. The course of recent events has been greatly determined by the military intervention of West African peacekeeping troops (ECOMOG). However, despite a supposed peace agreement that the elected government of Sierra Leone and rebels signed in 1999, fighting continues and the situation has not improved.

Evidence of Mortality

The conflict in Sierra Leone began in 1991. By the time of the 1992 coup d'etat, there were outbreaks of pertussis (whooping cough) and measles, and floods destroyed food crops. By the mid-1990s, half a million persons were displaced. Approximately 700,000 of Sierra Leone's population of 5 million are believed to have been internally displaced, particularly during 1998-1999, and 440,000 refugees have crossed the borders into Guinea and Liberia.

Prior to the hostilities, Sierra Leone already had the highest mortality rates in the world. Until recently, few NGOs had a presence in Sierra Leone, Africare being an exception. Today NGOs in Sierra Leone have unusually good coordination, and data is well shared. So estimates of mortality from the capital and major IDP areas (5,000-10,000 deaths) are fairly robust. Data from the hinterland and refugee camps, however, must be surmised. Estimates range from 20,000 to 50,000 additional deaths during the 1990s.

Estimates of Excess Mortality

Much of the killing, terrorism, and mortality secondary to forced displacement is unseen and, therefore, unrecorded and underestimated. The U.S. Office of Foreign Disaster Assistance (OFDA) has said it is impossible to make any estimates of mortality, reflecting the large gaps in information about most of the affected population. Nevertheless, its official situation report states that fighting in the 1990s has claimed at least 20,000 lives (Office of Foreign Disaster Assistance, 1999). Because this figure is not based on any review of the primary health care problems that followed the state collapse, forced migration, malnutrition, and economic damage, it is probably substantially inaccurate and an underestimate.

Multiple reports indicate that in three weeks in 1999, 5,000 people were killed in and around Freetown (United Nations Office for the Coordination of Humanitarian Affairs, 1999b). Thousands of civilians have been abducted in the movement of armies, and hundreds of children are missing and presumed to be abducted. It is hard to know what to infer from this type of disappearance data. As early as 1996, analysts believed that the war had already led to 25,000 deaths (Reno, 1998). So the true cumulative excess mortality rate could be at least 35,000 by now.

High rates of malnutrition have been found in northern districts, now that international agencies have access to these populations (United Nations Office for the Coordination of Humanitarian Affairs, 1999a). Many of the estimates of mortality are inferential, however, based on expected levels of childhood mortality given high rates of malnutrition and diarrhea.

Mortality Risk Factors

Most of the excess mortality is related to malnutrition, diarrhea, and communicable diseases. Much of the country had good immunization coverage in the past, and there was an apparent general reduction in vaccine-preventable diseases as well as diarrheal and respiratory diseases between the 1970s and early 1990s (Hodges and Williams, 1998).

One health risk that emerged in 1998 in Sierra Leone was limb amputation, perpetrated by rebels as a tactic of terror and retribution. Tens of thousands of persons have had arms or hands cut off, and no studies have yet estimated the case fatality rate from these injuries, which is likely to be substantial.

The presence or absence of aid agencies also appears to play a large role in which groups of people suffer excess mortality. Some of the largest IDP camps benefit from good public health programs by international NGOs. Where aid agencies had access, they had success in containing a measles epidemic (e.g., in the towns of Bo and Blama in early 1999).

As in other emergencies (i.e., Somalia and Ethiopia) the effectiveness of international aid to mitigate excess mortality in Sierra Leone appears to be cumulative—that is, it is better during the later stages than during the early stages, when risk of death was highest. Only now are aid agencies able to set up camps and access populations in need.

REFERENCES

Andersson, N., C. Palha da Sousa, and S. Paredes
   1995   Social cost of land mines in four countries: Afghanistan, Bosnia, Cambodia and Mozambique. *British Medical Journal* 311: 718-721.
Bennett, J.
   1999   Personal communication.
Borden, A., and R. Caplan
   1996   The former Yugoslavia: The war and the peace process. P. 203 in *SIPRI Yearbook 1996*. Oxford, UK: Oxford University Press.
Boss, L., E.W. Brink, and T. Dondero
   1986   Infant mortality and childhood nutritional status among Afghan refugees in Pakistan. *International Journal of Epidemiology* 16(4):556-560.
Brown, V., B. Reilley, M. Ferrir, and S. Manoncourt
   1996   Cholera outbreak during massive influx of Rwandan returnees in November, 1996. *Lancet* 349(9046):212.
Centers for Disease Control and Prevention
   1993   Status of public health in Bosnia and Herzegovina. *Morbidity and Mortality Weekly Report* 973:979-982.
Choudhry, V., I. Fazal, G. Aram, M. Choudhry, L.S. Arya, and M.S. Torpeki
   1989   Pattern of preventable diseases in Afghanistan: Suggestions to reduce the morbidity and mortality at IGICH. *Indian Pediatrics* 26(7):654-659.
Cohen, M.
   1996   *Afghanistan: Abandoned to Violence, Drugs, Hunger, Disease and Death.* Maryland: Bread for the World.
Cohen, R.
   1998   *Hearts Grown Brutal: Sagas of Sarajevo.* New York: Random House.
Coupland, R.
   1991   Injuries from antipersonnel mines: The experience of the International Committee of the Red Cross. *British Medical Journal* 303:1509-1512.
Cuny, F.C.
   1996   Refugees, displaced persons and the United Nations system. Pp. 187-211 in R. Caynes, and R. Williamson, *US Foreign Policy and the United Nations System.* New York: WW Norton.
Des Forges, A.
   1999   *Leave None to Tell the Story: Genocide in Rwanda.* New York: Human Rights Watch.

Dowell, S., A. Toko, C. Sita, R. Piarroux, A. Duerr, and B. Woodruff
    1995   Health and nutrition in centers for unaccompanied children: Experience from the
           1994 Rwandan refugee crisis. *Journal of the American Medical Association* 273:1802-
           1806.
European Union, World Food Programme, and United Nations Children's Fund
    1998   *Nutrition Survey of the Democratic People's Republic of Korea.* Geneva: European
           Union, World Food Programme, and UNICEF.
Gessner, B.
    1994   Mortality rates, causes of death, and health status among displaced and resident
           populations of Kabul, Afghanistan. *Journal of the American Medical Association*
           272:382-385.
Goma Epidemiology Group
    1995   Public health impact of Rwandan refugee crisis: What happened in Goma, Zaire
           in July 1994? *Lancet* 345:339-343.
Hodges, M., and R. Williams
    1998   Registered infant and under-five deaths in Freetown, Sierra Leone from 1987-1991
           and a comparison with 1969-1979. *West African Journal of Medicine* 17(2):95-98.
Horton, R.
    1999   Croatia and Bosnia: The imprints of war. *Lancet* 353(9170):2139-2144.
International Federation of the Red Cross and Red Crescent Societies
    1999   *World Disasters Report 1999.* Geneva: International Federation of Red Cross and
           Red Crescent Societies.
Ivker, R.
    1990   United Nations launches aid appeal as Afghanistan faces further disaster. *Lancet*
           351(9101):508.
Kenney, G.
    1995   The Bosnian calculation. *New York Times Magazine.* April 23:42-43.
Khalidi, N.A.
    1991   Afghanistan: demographic consequences of war, 1978-1987. *Central Asian Survey*
           10:101-126.
Lindenberg, M.
    1999   Complex emergencies and NGOs: The example of CARE. Pp. 211-246 in J. Lean-
           ing, S.M. Briggs, and L.C. Chen, eds. *Humanitarian Crises: The Medical and Public
           Health Response.* Cambridge, MA: Harvard University Press.
Maricevic, A., and M. Erceg
    1997   War injuries to the extremities. *Military Medicine* 162(12):808-811.
McDiarmid, J.
    1995   Deaths and injuries caused by landmines. *Lancet* 346(8983):1167.
Médecins Sans Frontières
    1995   Bosnia. In *Populations in Danger 1995.* Paris: Médecins Sans Frontières.
Minear, L., J. Clark, R. Cohen, D. Gallagher, I. Guest, and T. Weiss
    1994   *Humanitarian Action in the Former Yugoslavia: The UN's Role 1991-1993.* Occasional
           Paper #18.   Providence, RI and Washington, DC: Humanitarianism and War
           Project and the Refugee Policy Group.
Natsios, A.
    1999   *The Politics of Famine in North Korea.* Washington, DC: U.S. Institute of Peace.
Office of Foreign Disaster Assistance
    1999   *Sierra Leone Complex Emergency Fact Sheet 17.* Washington, DC: U.S. Agency for
           International Development, Office of Foreign Disaster Assistance.
Omaar, R., and A. de Waal
    1994   *Rwanda: Death, Despair and Defiance.* London: Africa Rights.

Pilsczek, F.

1996   Visiting doctor's perspective in Afghanistan. *Lancet* 348(9041):1566-1568.

Pretto, E.A., M. Begovic, and M. Begovic

1994   Emergency medical services during the siege of Sarajevo, Bosnia and Herzegovina: A preliminary report. *Pre-hospital and Disaster Medicine* 9(2 Suppl 1):S39-S45.

Prunier, G.

1995   *The Rwanda Crisis: History of a Genocide.* New York: Columbia University Press.

Reno, W.

1998   *Warlord Politics and African States.* Boulder, Colorado: Lynne Rienner Publishers.

Robinson, C., M. Lee, K. Hill, and G. Burnham

1999   Mortality in North Korean migrant households: A retrospective study. *Lancet* 354:291-295.

Sliwinski, M.

1988   The decimation of Afghanistan. *Orbis* 33(Winter):39-56.

United Nations Office for the Coordination of Humanitarian Affairs.

1999a *1999 Mid-Term Review and Revision of United Nations Consolidated Inter-Agency Appeal for Sierra Leone.* New York: Office for the Coordination of Humanitarian Affairs.

1999b *Integrated Regional Information Network for West Africa.* News bulletin.

Wallensteen, P., and M. Sollenberg

1998   Armed conflicts and regional conflict complexes, 1989-97. *Journal of Peace Research* 35(5):621-634.

Weiss, T.

1999   *Military-Civilian Interactions: Intervening in Humanitarian Crises.* Lanham, MD: Rowman and Littlefield Publishers, Inc.

2

The Evolution of Mortality Among Rwandan Refugees in Zaire Between 1994 and 1997

Dominique Legros, Christophe Paquet, and Pierre Nabeth

INTRODUCTION

The civil war and the genocide that occurred in Rwanda between April and July 1994 killed an estimated 500,000 to 800,000 people. As a consequence, approximately 1 million Rwandans were internally displaced and 1.2 to 1.5 million fled to neighboring countries. Among the latter, probably 1 million settled in Eastern Zaire, in camps located in the Kivu provinces, along the border with their country of origin.

The influx of refugees in Goma, in the North Kivu province of Zaire, between July 14 and July 18, 1994 was considerable: between 500,000 and 850,000 persons, mostly from the Hutu ethnic group, crossed the border in a 5-day period (Millwood, 1996). During the first weeks of the emergency the mortality rates were very high, but very rapidly, by September 1994, after huge resources had been channelled to the area, the situation stabilized and mortality rates fell dramatically.

In the following period, most of the external assistance consisted of improving the health situation of the refugees by trying to reach international standards, particularly in terms of water supply, latrine construction, and food distribution. However, the situation remained very unsafe as the former Rwandan army (Forces Armées Rwandaises, or FAR) and the Interhamwe militia were active in the camps, preparing for military action. Protesting against insecurity and the indirect support they perceived was being given to the perpetrators of the genocide, some agencies withdrew all their personnel and assistance in November 1994.

In spite of this spectacular action, the situation remained unchanged in the camps until the emergence of the Alliance des Forces Démocratiques de Libération du Congo-Zaire (AFDL) movement in September 1996 in South Kivu. Laurent D. Kabila led this movement of rebellion against the Zairean state with the support of the governments of Uganda, Rwanda, and Burundi. The support to Kabila was a good opportunity for the government of Rwanda to eliminate the threat at its Western border represented by the refugee camps of Kivu.

In an attempt to evacuate the camps and force the refugees back to Rwanda, AFDL and its allies attacked the camps of Kivu between October and November 1996. As a result, around 900,000 refugees went back to their country of origin, while the remaining (including the ex-FAR) refugees fled into Zaire in an attempt to escape the AFDL forces which were heading towards Kinshasa. For some of them, this second forced migration in their country of asylum would last until May 1997 and bring them into Congo-Brazzaville after a trip of 1,500 kilometers. During their trip, these refugees faced extremely harsh conditions of living and were continuously pursued and attacked by the AFDL forces. In a few places, like in Tingi Tingi camp or along the Ubundu-Kisangani axis, they were able to settle down for some weeks, and external aid was provided until the camps were attacked. But most of the time, the access to this population was almost non-existent and very little information on their situation was available.

The purpose of our study was to review the several acute phases experienced by the Rwandan refugees from the first influx in Kivu in July 1994 until the settlement in the camps in Congo-Brazzaville in May 1997, concentrating on the ways in which mortality figures were collected. The objectives were to examine the importance of mortality data in complex emergency situations and to analyze the feasibility of the organization of a basic surveillance system in the most precarious conditions. Our goal was also to underline the limitations of the retrospective mortality surveys and the caution required in the extrapolation of their results.

MORTALITY DURING THE GOMA INFLUX

The refugees settled down initially in Goma town and later in Kibumba and Katale camps, situated north of the town, and in Mugunga camp to the west (Figure 2-1). During the initial emergency phase, the occurrence of major cholera and dysentery outbreaks and the precarious environmental conditions resulted in high mortality rates, which were recorded by a retrospective survey and a dead body collection system.

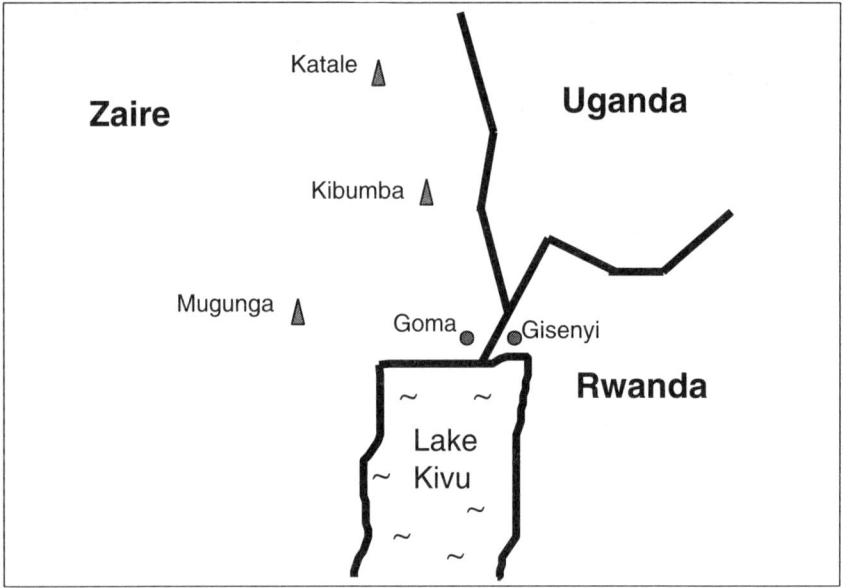

FIGURE 2-1 Location of the refugee camps in North Kivu. Not drawn to scale.

Methods

Surveillance System

From the first days of the intervention of the international agencies, emphasis was put on mortality and morbidity data collection. As the ground where most refugees settled was hard volcanic rock, the digging of graves was almost impossible, and dead bodies were left along the roads and tracks or in public places. A dead body collection system was therefore organized using trucks for burial in mass graves. It provided records of numbers of bodies collected per day.

A mapping exercise was performed in each camp. The geographical limits of the camps were first estimated, as a whole and by zones of shelter density (low, medium, and high), using a geographical position-ing system (GPS). This gave an estimate of the surface of the camp. Within each zone of shelter density, squares of 25 meters by 25 meters were selected at random.   The number of persons living within these squares was counted. This gave an estimate of the population density per square meter by zone, which, when multiplied by the area of each zone, gave a rough estimate of the total population of the camps.

The population figures were also estimated from the number of doses delivered during a mass vaccination campaign against meningitis, and from the vaccine coverage evaluated during a subsequent vaccine coverage survey.

Retrospective Mortality Surveys

Population retrospective mortality surveys were conducted in Katale, Kibumba, and Mugunga camps from August 4 to August 14, 1994. These surveys were designed to estimate the average mortality rate in each camp since the arrival of the refugees, and to evaluate the nutritional status of children under age five.

Each survey was conducted using a two-stage cluster sampling method. Within each camp, 30 clusters of 20 households were selected at random. Household composition and information on mortality since arrival in Zaire were obtained by interviewing the head of the family.

Results

The populations of Katale, Kibumba, and Mugunga camps were estimated at 80,000, 180,000, and 150,000, respectively. Some refugees had settled down in Goma town, to the north of Katale, and to the west of Mugunga and were not counted.

The first case of cholera in Goma was diagnosed on July 20, 1994. This led to a major cholera outbreak of 58,000 to 80,000 cases within a month after the influx (Goma Epidemiology Group, 1995). The cholera outbreak was still active when an outbreak of bloody diarrhea, due to *Shigella dysenteriae* type 1, erupted in the first days of August and persisted in all the camps until November 1994.

These successive outbreaks contributed greatly to the unprecedented mortality rates observed during the first weeks of the emergency. A total of 48,347 dead bodies were buried between July 14 and August 14 (Goma Epidemiology Group, 1995). Although this might be an underestimation of the true figures (because of private burials), the estimate of 50,000 deaths occurring during the first month of the emergency has been generally accepted (Millwood, 1996).

The average daily crude mortality rates (CMRs) estimated by the retrospective mortality surveys were two to three times higher than the death rates reported from previous complex emergency situations in Ethiopia and Sudan (1985), Somalia (1992), and Iraq (1991) (Table 2-1). According to the surveys, 85 to 90 percent of the deaths reported were related to diarrheal diseases. In Katale, adults and children under age five appeared equally affected by diarrhea-related deaths (Paquet and Van Soest, 1994).

TABLE 2-1 Comparison of Crude Mortality Rate Estimates Derived from Dead Body Count and from Population Surveys, Goma to Zaire, July - August 1994

Survey or Count	Survey Period (July 14 to)	Estimated Population	Crude Mortality Rate (per 10,000 per day)	Percentage of Population Dying During the Period [95 % confidence interval]
Katale survey	August 4	80,000	41.3	8.3 [7.1–9.5]
Kibumba survey	August 9	180,000	28.1	7.3 [6.2–8.6]
Mugunga survey	August 13	150,000	29.4	9.1 [7.9–10.3]
Body count (all areas)	August 14	500,000–850,000	31.2–19.5	9.7–6.0

Source: Goma Epidemiology Group (1995).

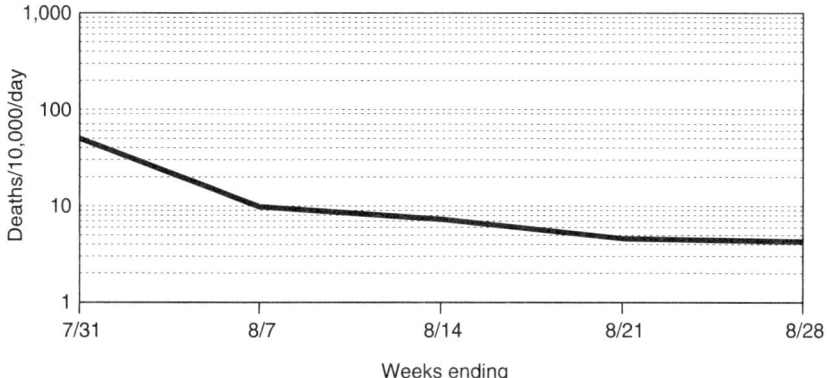

FIGURE 2-2   Crude daily mortality rates per week, Katale Camp, Goma, Zaire, July-August 1994.

Surveillance and survey data were consistent. Depending on population estimates, 6 to 10 percent of the refugees who arrived in Goma between July 14 and July 18, 1994 died within a month after their arrival. The high mortality rates recorded, and explained almost entirely by the outbreaks of cholera and dysentery, confirm the occurrence of a public health disaster of major proportions.

However, within some weeks, CMRs declined sharply, and by the end of August was estimated at 3.0 per 10,000 per day in Katale, for instance (Figure 2-2). This result can be related to the international community's huge response to the Goma crisis. Even if the level of performance of some agencies was poor and their impact on the crisis questionable (if not negative), it is generally accepted that, overall, the results of the humanitarian intervention were impressive. In particular, the speed with which enormous quantities of water of good quality were supplied to most camps was commendable and had a key role in the control of the outbreaks of diarrheal diseases.

MORTALITY IN TINGI TINGI

The attacks of the refugee camps in Kivu by the troops of the AFDL in October and November 1996 marked the beginning of a period during which the humanitarian situation of the refugees deteriorated. According to figures from the United Nations High Commissioner for Refugees (UNHCR), over 340,000 refugees remained in Zaire, hiding in the forests of Kivu, or fleeing west ahead of the advancing front line. From October 1996 until June 1997, the refugees were victims of intimidation, ill treatment, and killings, and were denied adequate protection and assistance. In mid-December 1996, groups of refugees who had been forced out of the camps in Eastern Zaire and had since been missing, resurfaced at Tingi Tingi, Shabunda, and Amisi camps, in Maniéma province, where they received assistance until those camps were also attacked on February 28, 1997. Later on, and except during a short period in the south of Kisangani, the humanitarian agencies had almost no access to these populations until they reached Congo-Brazzaville.

Methods

A surveillance system was established in Tingi Tingi, which provided mortality data from the beginning of the intervention (Nabeth, 1997). The number of deaths was computed on a daily basis by age group: under five and five and over. Deaths were recorded from the hospital, the intensive feeding center, and the cholera isolation unit. In addition, a "grave watcher" had been hired to report the number of new graves dug per day and the place of the death (e.g., hospital or home). A mapping of the camp was conducted initially to estimate the population figures. Later on, a registration system was set up for new arrivals.

Results

The population of Tingi Tingi was estimated at 80,000 persons, of which 12,000 (15 percent) were children under five years old (Nabeth, 1997). From December 18, 1996 to February 26, 1997, a total of 1,703 deaths were recorded by the surveillance system, of which 831 (48.8 percent) occurred among children under five. Over the period, the average crude and under-five mortality rates were 3.0 and 9.8 per 10,000 per day, respectively. Although a phenomenon of double counting might have occurred in some cases, because of the double sources of information, the observed rates were well above the limits generally admitted for situations out of control (2.0 and 4.0 per 10,000 per day for the crude and under-five mortality rates, respectively).

The trends showed a clear and constant deterioration of the health status of the refugees over time (Figure 2-3) (Nabeth et al., 1997b). This was primarily due to the absence of adequate food supplies. Between December 27, 1996 (the first day of food distribution), and January 24, 1997, a daily average of 900 kilocalories per person was provided to the refugees (UNHCR recommends a daily ration of 2,100 kilocalories per person per day). The high mortality rates were also explained by the development of a dysentery outbreak followed by a cholera outbreak (Nabeth, 1997).

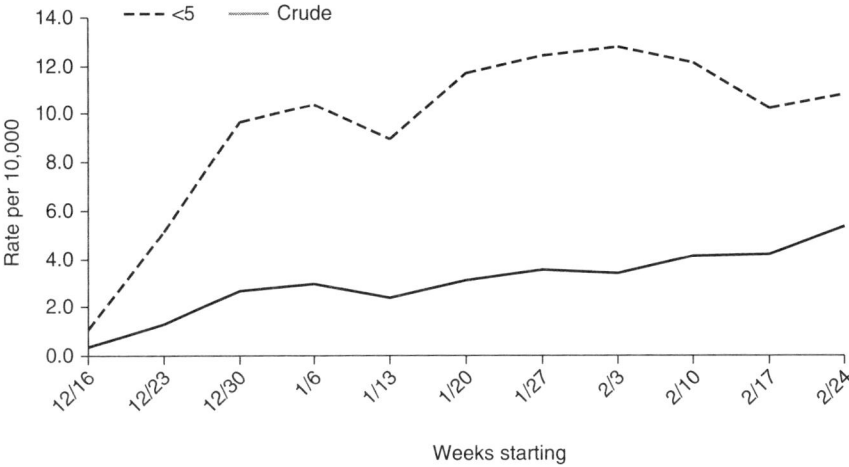

FIGURE 2-3 Average daily mortality rates per week among refugees in Tingi Tingi, Maniéma, Zaire, December 1996-February 1997.

MORTALITY IN THE CAMPS ALONG THE UBUNDU-KISANGANI RAILWAY

By the end of February 1997, the AFDL forces reached Tingi Tingi, and most of the refugees fled to the west, in the direction of Ubundu and Kisangani. In late March 1997, the first groups of refugees reached Ubundu, 100 kilometers south of Kisangani. From there, they moved north along the railway to Kisangani. AFDL did not allow them passage through this town, and by mid-April, refugees had set up camps at several locations along the railway line from Ubundu to Kisangani.

Methods

In spite of the very difficult conditions and limited access to the refugee populations, temporary hospitals and dispensaries were set up. They allowed the collection of mortality data on a daily basis, by age group (under-five and five and over). In addition, a network of community health workers was rapidly created in Kasese. Population figures were estimated empirically.

Results

Overall, it was estimated that 80,000-85,000 refugees had settled in multiple camps along the railway line. Overcrowding and poor sanitation made the living conditions in the camps particularly difficult, and, as expected in those conditions, the estimated mortality rates were extremely high. By mid-April, 1,581 deaths had been officially registered since the beginning of the month (the CMR was 11.6 to 12.4 per 10,000 per day). Access to the refugees remained very limited and logistic difficulties were considerable. The camps were attacked during the last week of April 1997. Some refugees continued their flight to the west, some hid in the forest and came back some days later, and many disappeared.

Groups of refugees were again located in May 1997 in Mbandaka and Wenji, on the eastern bank of the Congo River. After a final attack on the camps, they crossed over towards Congo-Brazzaville.

MORTALITY IN NDJOUNDOU AND LOUKOLÉLA, CONGO-BRAZZAVILLE

By mid-May 1997, several hundred Rwandan refugees were identified in Congo-Brazzaville in a swampy area located 600 kilometers north of Brazzaville along the Oubangui River. They had settled in camps located in three villages: Loukoléla, Liranga, and Ndjoundou.

Methods

Surveillance System

An epidemiological surveillance system was rapidly established in all the camps. The number of deaths was collected on a daily basis from the hospital registers. In addition, right from the beginning, the local authorities organized a registration system of the new arrivals and assigned a separate cemetery to the refugee population with a system to register deaths. A census was carried out prior to a general food distribution. A list of all the families present in the camp was therefore available.

Retrospective Mortality Survey

A retrospective mortality survey was conducted in July 1997 in Ndjoundou with the objective of reconstituting *a posteriori* the group of origin in the camps of Kivu and of documenting the sequence of events that occurred in that population since the attacks at the end of 1996 (Nabeth et al., 1997a). A systematic random sample of 266 families was selected from the list of families of Ndjoundou. One person per family was interviewed. The questions were about the extended family while in Kivu (persons living together, not necessarily under the same roof), and included: the camp of origin in Kivu, the number of persons in the family while in Kivu with their age and sex, the date of departure from the camp in Kivu, the names of the places where the family stopped for at least several days and, for each of those places, the members of the family present and the events explaining the absence of the other members. The following events were documented: death (by illness, accident or murder), repatriation to Rwanda, spontaneous return to Rwanda, and disappearance. Only confirmed deaths were recorded as such; if the death was simply assumed, the person was reported missing.

Results

At the end of June 1997, the total population of Loukoléla was estimated at 6,400 persons and that of Ndjoundou at 3,370 persons (1,650 families). At that time (that is, one and a half months after the arrival of the first refugees), the mortality rate recorded by the surveillance system in both camps was below 1.0 per 10,000 per day; for the last week of June the average daily CMR was 0.2 in Loukoléla and 0.5 in Ndjoundou (Figure 2-4). The main causes of death were typical for refugee situations: malaria and diarrhea (including cholera) in the five and above age group, and malaria, acute respiratory infections, diarrhea and malnutrition among the under-five age group.

A total of 266 heads of families were interviewed during the retrospective mortality survey in Ndjoundou. They represented a population of 530 persons (15.7 percent of the total population of the camp). Men aged 20 to 39 were clearly over-represented in the sample (Figure 2-5).

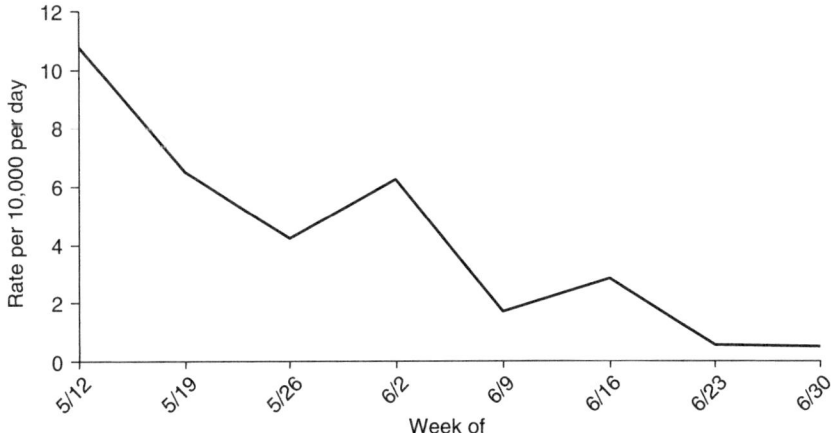

FIGURE 2-4 Average daily crude mortality rate per week, Ndjoundou, Congo-Brazzaville, May-June 1997.

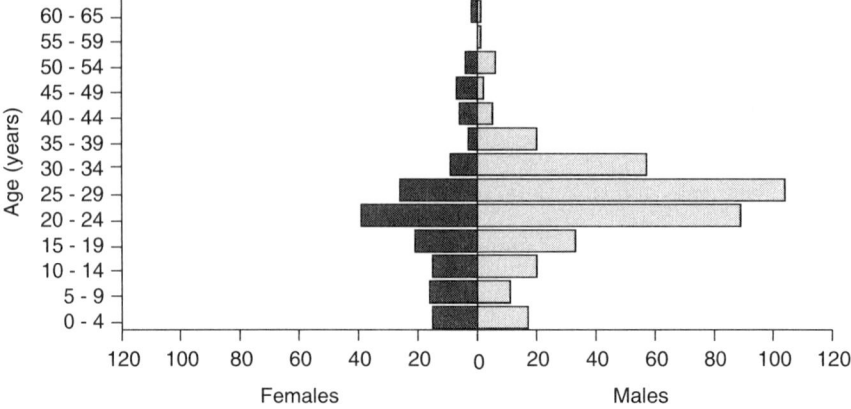

FIGURE 2-5 Distribution by age and sex of the population of the sample (N=530), Ndjoundou, Congo-Brazzaville, July 1997.

But this was also the case in the entire population of Ndjoundou (Table 2-2), and in the initial group reconstituted from the information collected during the survey (Figure 2-6). The 530 persons included in the sample in Ndjoundou came from an estimated group of 3,121 persons in the camps of Kivu. Of this initial group, 651 persons died (20.9 percent, with a 95 percent confidence interval of 19.5-22.3) and 1,857 disappeared (59.5 percent, with a 95 percent confidence interval of 57.8-61.2) during their trip through Zaire. Most of the persons who died were killed (Table 2-3).

TABLE 2-2   Age and Sex Distribution in the Sample and in the Total Population of the Camp, Ndjoundou, Congo-Brazzaville, July 1997

Population Parameter		Sample (n = 530)	Camp (n = 3370)
Sex	Male	367	2429
	Female	163	941
	Sex Ratio (Males/Females)	2.25	2.58
Age (Years)	Median	24.0	24.0
	Number (Percentage)	32	263
	under Five Years of Age	(7.9%)	(8.5 %)
Age of Males	Median	25.0	25.0
Age of Females	Median	22.0	21.0

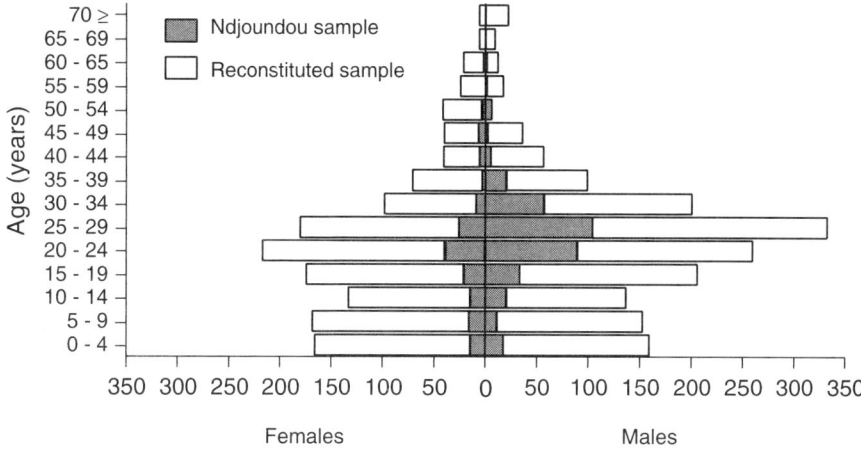

FIGURE 2-6 Distribution by age and sex of the sample in Ndjoundou (N=530) and of the reconstituted sample (N=3,121), Ndjoundou, Congo-Brazzaville, July 1997.

The trip of the refugees through Zaire was reconstituted from the interviews. Each family had its own itinerary, but four gathering places were clearly identified: Shanje (for the refugees coming from the Bukavu area), Tingi Tingi, Ubundu, and Wenji.

It was also possible to find the places and the dates when refugees were killed or disappeared. A high proportion of the population living in the camps of Mugunga, Sake, Shanje, Ubundu-Obilo, and Wenji were killed or disappeared during the various attacks (Table 2-4).

When considering the evolution of the size of the reconstituted group over time, three periods showed a sudden drop in the number of refugees remaining in the group. These periods corresponded to the months following the attacks of the camps in Kivu (November 1996), along the railway from Ubundu to Kisangani (April 1997), and in Wenji (May 1997) (Figure 2-7). However, since these projections included the refugees who died or disappeared, more accurate figures might be provided by considering the number of deaths only. It was possible, from the results of the interviews, to calculate the crude and under-five mortality rates by period of time. Again, three peaks of mortality were observed corresponding to the same periods (Figure 2-8). The average daily crude and under-five mortality rate over the period were 15.5 and 18.2 per 10,000 per day, respectively.

TABLE 2-3 Distribution of the Events Occurring Among Rwandan Refugees During Their Flight from Kivu to Congo-Brazzaville, Ndjoundou, Congo-Brazzaville, July 1997

Events	N	Percentage	95 Percent Confidence Interval
Event Explaining the Absence:			
Disappearance	1857	59.5	57.8-61.2
Death:			
Murder	615	19.7	18.3-21.1
Illness	24	0.8	0.5-1.1
Accident	12	0.4	0.2-0.7
Spontaneous Return	33	1.0	0.7-1.5
Repatriation	34	1.1	0.8-1.5
Present:			
Present in Ndjoundou	530	17.0	15.7-18.3
Present in Another Camp	16	0.5	0.3-0.8
Total	**3121**	**100.0**	**N/A**

TABLE 2-4 Proportion of the Refugee Population Killed or Disappeared by Place, Ndjoundou, Congo-Brazzaville, July 1997

| Place | Population | Killed | | | Disappeared | | |
		N	Percent	95 Percent Confidence Interval	N	Percent	95 Percent Confidence Interval
Mugunga	211	33	15.6	11.2–21.0	57	27.0	21.3–33.3
Sake	447	55	12.3	9.5–15.6	136	30.4	26.3–34.8
Shanje	1597	84	5.3	4.2–6.4	512	32.1	29.8–34.4
Walikale	686	38	5.5	4.0–7.4	28	4.1	2.8–5.8
Tingi-Tingi	1557	43	2.8	2.0–3.7	104	6.7	5.5–8.0
Ubundu	1336	17	1.3	0.8–2.0	207	15.5	13.6–17.5
Obiro	665	46	6.9	5.2–9.0	136	20.5	17.5–23.6
Ikela	397	4	1.0	0.3–2.4	22	5.5	3.6–8.1
Boende	224	32	14.3	10.2–9.3	25	11.2	7.5–15.8
Ingende	209	0	0.0	N/A	2	1.0	0.2–3.1
Wenji	954	130	13.6	11.6–15.9	288	30.2	27.3–33.2
Unknown		133			340		
Total		615			1857		

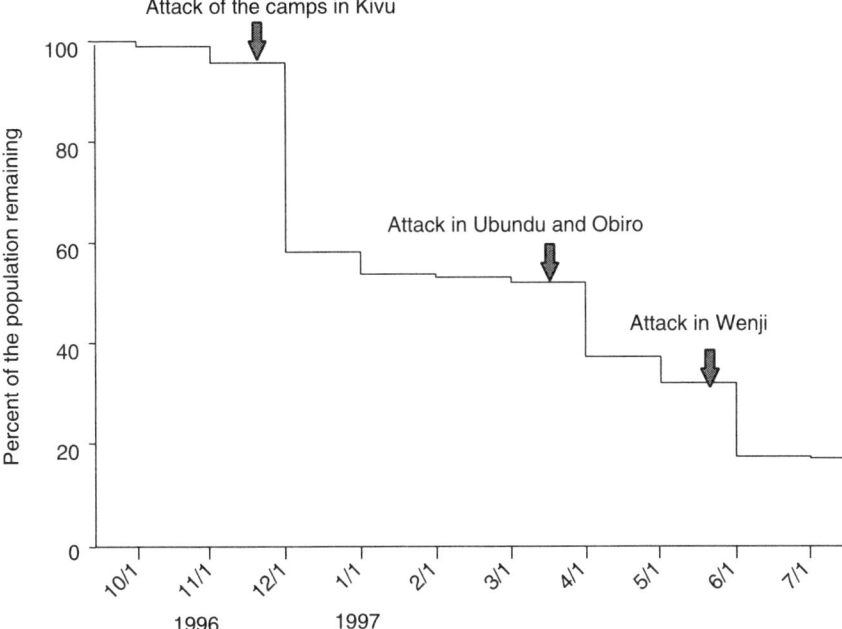

FIGURE 2-7 Evolution of the size of the reconstituted group of refugees from Kivu over time, Ndjoundou, Congo-Brazzaville, July 1997.

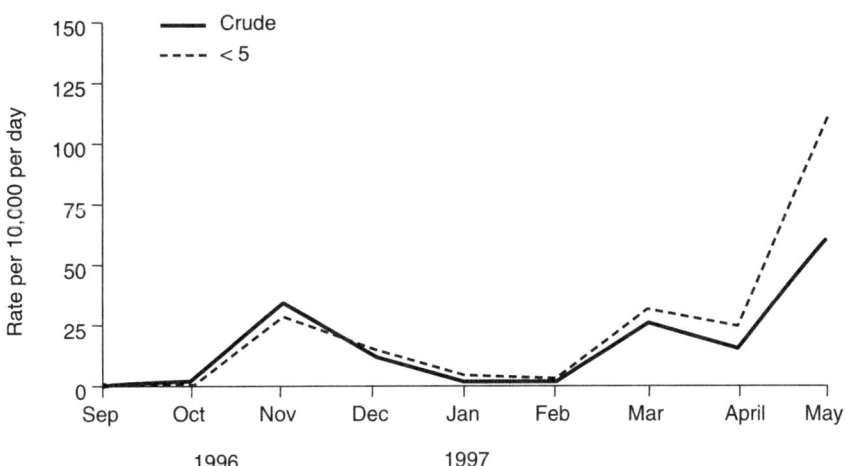

FIGURE 2-8 Average crude and under-five daily mortality rates per month, Rwandan refugees, Ndjoundou, Congo-Brazzaville, July 1997.

DISCUSSION

Mortality rates are the most useful health indicators for assessing the seriousness of emergency situations. Two methods are recommended for measuring mortality in a refugee population (both were used for the Rwandan refugees in Zaire): the retrospective mortality surveys and the ongoing surveillance system. Either method gives estimates of the crude and under-five mortality rates that can then be compared to the expected crude mortality rate in developing countries (on average, 25 per 1,000 per year, or 0.6 per 10,000 per day). A situation is considered an emergency when the CMR exceeds 1 per 10,000 per day. Reference rates in the under-five age group are double that found in the general population; it is considered to be an emergency situation when the under-five mortality rate is above 2 per 10,000 per day.

The implementation of a surveillance system and the collection of population figures are priority actions that should be undertaken right from the beginning of an emergency situation. Some of our examples (Tingi Tingi, Ubundu, and the camps along the railway to Kisangani) demonstrated that this was feasible, even in the most difficult situations. The information can come from different sources, depending on the places: dead body collection, grave watchers, or hospital and therapeutic feeding center registers. Whatever the origin of the information, biases can affect both the population figures (frequent overestimation) and the number of deaths reported (over- or undernotification, delay in reporting, etc.). In emergency situations these biases are difficult to control, and, therefore, the objective of surveillance in this context can only be to monitor trends over time, and not to provide exact figures. Decisions made and information communicated must be based on these trends rather than on isolated results.

Retrospective mortality surveys should be conducted (and sometimes repeated) when no surveillance data are available, such as occurred in the camps of Kivu in August 1994, to document events which occurred during the migration, such as in Congo-Brazzaville in 1997. The latter is of particular interest because of the historical information it can provide. On the other hand, retrospective mortality surveys also have limitations and caution is required in the extrapolation of their results.

The mortality rate obtained from a retrospective survey is always an average over the recall period, and confidence intervals must always be added around the central value. If the recall period is long, the average rate might not represent what is actually happening at the time of the survey and this could lead to inappropriate decisions. Long recall period will also affect the precision of the data collected. Conversely, if recall period is short, there is a risk of measuring a very specific event which might not be representative of the overall situation. Short recall period also allows fewer events (deaths) to be recorded, and thus reduces the precision of the estimate (or implies the need for a bigger sample size to get the same level of precision). In any case, mortality data collected from retrospective surveys should be used with caution for forecasting purposes, especially when figures are abnormally high. Peaks of mortality documented during communicable disease outbreaks or nutrition emergencies, for example, often reflect what is happening in the most vulnerable groups of the population. Once these groups have been affected, there is often a change in mortality pattern.

The sampling technique and the questionnaire are two other potential domains of weakness of retrospective mortality surveys. The sampling technique refers almost always to a two-stage cluster sampling method. In this method, only the first sampling unit is selected at random within the cluster, while the following units are selected on a proximity basis. The method has only been validated for vaccine coverage surveys and might not be suited for mortality surveys if the mortality patterns are correlated, in any way, with the geographical location of the houses within the cluster. This will increase the cluster effect, and therefore reduce the precision of the estimate, everything else being equal. Furthermore, the sampling unit in mortality surveys is the household, but inferences are made on individuals.

The questionnaires used during retrospective mortality surveys are much less elaborate than the ones used for verbal autopsies. Their validity has never been evaluated. They are usually built on the spot, and are often applied by inexperienced and rapidly trained personnel.

Finally, retrospective mortality surveys can be affected by a survival bias. This bias probably occurred during the survey conducted in Ndjoundou in Congo-Brazzaville in July 1997. In this case, and given the proportion of the initial group who died during the trip through Zaire, it is very likely that many families disappeared completely and were therefore not interviewed. This was partly taken into account by considering the extended African family in Kivu instead of the nuclear family. But we still might get a biased estimate of the true mortality rates, either by underestimation (i.e., survival bias) or by overestimation (i.e., multiple reporting of the deaths).

For all these reasons, the interpretation of retrospective mortality surveys must be very cautious. These surveys are conducted in difficult conditions and, most of the time, by few and inexperienced personnel. Recall and survival biases are both likely. The validity of the questionnaires and of the sampling techniques has never been evaluated. The extrapolation of the results to other camps and other situations (for instance to refugees with a different history of exodus) is very hazardous.

To our knowledge, the retrospective mortality survey conducted in Ndjoundou camp in Congo-Brazzaville was the first of this type in a refugee setting. Since then, the same method has been used to document the exodus of Kosovar refugees in Albania and Montenegro in 1999 (Brown et al., 2000; Physicians for Human Rights, 1999). The testimony and advocacy activities, favored and reinforced by the validity of the information collected during these surveys, will obviously not protect *a posteriori* the victims of injustice, but they can have an impact on the prevention of violence against vulnerable civil populations in the future. Retrospective surveys of the history of migration should be multiplied during complex emergencies. At the same time, their methodology should be assessed and refined.

REFERENCES

Brown, V., W. Perea, G. Godain, E. Dachy, and M. Valenciano
    2000   Kosovar refugees in Montenegro and Albania. *Refuge* 18(5):43-45.
Goma Epidemiology Group
    1995   Public health impact of Rwandan refugee crisis: What happened in Goma, Zaire, in July 1994? *Lancet* 345:339-344.
Millwood, D., ed.
    1996   *The International Response to Conflict and Genocide: Lessons from the Rwanda Experience. Humanitarian Aid and Effects.* Geneva: Steering Committee of the Joint Evaluation of Emergency Assistance to Rwanda.
Nabeth, P.
    1997   Compte-rendu de mission à Tingi Tingi, Zaïre. Internal report, Epicentre, Paris, January 1997.
Nabeth, P., C. Ndayambaje, A. Croisier, and M. Pédari
    1997a Histoire des réfugiés rwandais ayant fui les camps du Kivu, Zaïre, de septembre 1996 à juin 1997. Résultats d'une enquête effectuée parmi les survivants du camp de Ndjoundou, au Congo. Internal report, Epicentre, Paris, September 1997.
Nabeth, P., B. Vasset, P. Guérin, B. Doppler, and M. Tectonidis
    1997b Health situation of refugees in eastern Zaire. *Lancet* 349:1031-1032.
Paquet, C., and M. Van Soest
    1994   Mortality and malnutrition among Rwandan refugees in Zaire. *Lancet* 344:823-824.
Physicians for Human Rights
    1999   *War Crimes in Kosovo: A Population-Based Assessment of Human Rights Violations of Kosovar Albanians by Serb Forces.* Boston: Physicians for Human Rights.

3

Famine, Mortality, and Migration: A Study of North Korean Migrants in China

W. Courtland Robinson, Myung Ken Lee, Kenneth Hill, and Gilbert Burnham

> This is a famine in slow motion. People cope year after year and proba-
> bly a lot drop off. But the totality is very hard to gauge.
>
> —*Official, UN World Food Program (November 1998).*

INTRODUCTION

It would be a profound understatement to say that accurate, up-to-
date information on the Democratic People's Republic of Korea (DPRK) is
limited. The latest census, conducted in 1993, recorded a population of
21,213,378, of whom males numbered 10,329,699 and females 10,883,679
(United Nations Department of Economic and Social Affairs, 1998). The
estimated midyear population for 1996 was 22,466,000, assuming an annual growth rate of 1.6 percent. The United Nations (UN) estimate of the
crude birth rate for 1990-1995 was 21.8 per 1,000 and the estimated crude
death rate (CDR) was 5.5 per 1,000; therefore, the crude rate of natural
increase was 16.3. Infant mortality was estimated at 24.4 deaths of children under one year old per 1,000 live births. Eberstadt and Banister
(1992), factoring in uncounted males in the military, estimated the 1996
midyear population of North Korea at 23,906,122 and the 1998 midyear
population at 24,721,312.

Given the country's hardships in recent years, however, the question
of how many people are living—or have died—in North Korea is
shrouded in greater mystery than ever. The deterioration of the North
Korean economy since 1990, a disastrous combination of flooding in 1995

and 1996, and drought in 1997 have brought on a severe food crisis in the reclusive, communist nation that has placed millions of people at risk of starvation. Infusions of international food aid since 1996 are believed to have helped stabilize the situation, at least in certain areas and among targeted populations, but the crisis does not seem to have passed. Efforts to gauge the effects of this crisis, however, have been hampered by the North Korean government's reluctance to permit randomized surveys of morbidity and mortality.

A nutritional assessment mission to the DPRK undertaken by the World Food Program (WFP) in August 1997 found a 16.5 percent prevalence of wasting (<-2 Z-scores weight-for-height) and a 38.2 percent prevalence of stunting (<-2 Z-scores height-for-age) in a nonrandom sample of 3,695 children under 7 years of age in 42 selected nurseries and kindergartens from 19 counties in 5 provinces. The WFP assessment noted that "a prevalence of wasting greater than 15 percent is considered a serious situation and suggests that mortality rates have already increased" (Katona-Apte and Mokdad, 1998). In September 1998, WFP collaborated with the United Nations Children's Fund (UNICEF) and the European Union to conduct a randomized survey of 1,762 children in 3,600 households in 30 North Korean counties. This survey found 15.6 percent of children aged 6 months to 7 years to be wasted, 62.3 percent stunted, and 60.6 percent moderately or severely underweight (European Union et al., 1998). The authors of the 1997 WFP study concluded that

> The chronic and cumulative shortage of food, the shortages of basic medicine and fuel, the damage to the infrastructure from floods, and the difficult economic circumstances of the DPRK pose substantial challenges to improving the nutritional status of its children. On the other hand, the presence of the PDS [Public Distribution System], the evident order and discipline in DPRK society, the universal access to health care, the dedication of the care providers and the high literacy rate augur well for the likelihood of successful resolution of the crisis if adequate food, medication and training can be made available (Katona-Apte and Mokdad, 1998).

Other assessments were not so sanguine. Frustrated by the DPRK's unwillingness to permit random sample surveys or independent interviewing of the population, some organizations began to look to the Chinese border where North Koreans had been crossing in search of food. In July 1997, World Vision interviewed 33 individuals at the China/North Korea border (19 of whom were North Korean and 14 of whom were from either China or Russia) and concluded that mortality averaged 15 percent in the northern provinces. "This famine," said the World Vision report, "may well be much more severe than any news reports have indicated" (World Vision, 1997).

In June 1998, a private South Korean organization called the Korean

Buddhist Sharing Movement (KBSM) released a report on the North Korean food crisis based on interviews with North Korean migrants in China. Summarizing results from five phases of interviews conducted between September 1997 and May 1998, the KBSM study reported that "the [cumulative] mortality rate over the last 2 years and 9 months (August 1995-April 1998) has reached 27.0 percent...The mortality rate for 1996 was at 8.86 percent [88.6 per 1,000] and for 1997, 19.60 percent [196 per 1,000]." The survey also found that the birth rate to sample families was 0.93 percent [9.3 per 1,000] in 1996 and 0.86 percent [8.6 per 1,000] in 1997. "We have determined," the report stated, "that the worst famine in human history is now transpiring in North Korea" (Korean Buddhist Sharing Movement, 1998).

Concerned by these accounts but unable to assess the reliability of their findings, a U.S. nongovernmental organization (NGO) active in North Korean humanitarian relief, Mercy Corps International, invited the Johns Hopkins School of Public Health to undertake its own study of North Korean migrants in China. In the past five years, significant numbers of North Koreans have been moving across the Chinese border in search of food for themselves and their families. It is estimated that between 50,000 and 150,000 North Koreans are staying temporarily in China, principally in Yanbian Korean Autonomous Prefecture, which is home to nearly 1 million Korean-Chinese. Bound by ties of kinship and ethnicity, Korean-Chinese families along the border and throughout the prefecture have tried to help their relatives with food, shelter, cash, and clothing.

STUDY DESIGN

The Hopkins study had two specific research objectives, one substantive and the other methodological. The first was to develop a demographic profile of North Korean migrants in order to understand better the phenomenon of migration in the context of food crisis. The second objective was to explore the use of indirect estimation techniques in calculating mortality and other vital rates. In March 1998, we distributed a self-administered questionnaire to approximately 200 local aid networks in Yanbian, asking them about their assistance to North Koreans. Of the 102 networks that responded, just over half (n=57) reported that they assisted North Korean migrants. From the list of 57 active sites, we drew a stratified sample of 18 sites, selecting at least one site from each of the eight counties of Yanbian Prefecture: Yanji, Hunchun, Yungjung, Tumen, Hwaryong, Ando, Wangchung, and Donwha. The border counties of Yanji, Hunchun, Yungjung, Tumen, and Hwaryong received multiple random picks proportional to the number of active sites in the county.

In May 1998, one Korean-Chinese interviewer was selected for each site and provided with several days of individual training, including such topics as survey methodology, techniques for good interviewing, and questionnaire formats. We also employed three field supervisors to provide ongoing monitoring of the interviews and checking of the questionnaires. In June, each interviewer conducted at least 10 practice interviews using a pretest form of the questionnaire. Based on feedback from the interviewers, the questionnaire was revised and training was provided for the new forms. Surveying began in early July and concluded at the end of September 1998, covering a three-month period. Results from that study were published in the July 24, 1999 issue of *The Lancet* (Robinson et al., 1999).

From July to September 1999, interviews were conducted with an additional 381 North Korean arrivals at eight sites along the border. These sites, all of which had participated in the 1998 study, were selected based on: their willingness to participate for another year, and the presence of at least moderate levels of cross-border arrivals. All North Korean respondents were assured that the interview was voluntary and confidential. We interviewed only migrants who were 18 or older and only one member of a family travelling together. No incentives were given to respondents, although interviewers received a small monthly stipend. It is estimated that between 80 and 90 percent of all arrivals at the 8 sites were interviewed during the 3-month period with a nonresponse rate of less than 5 percent.

Respondents were asked to provide a list of all household members who were alive as of January 1995 (we defined a household as people who normally live together and share the same cooking facility) and to report births, deaths, in-migrations (>1 month), and out-migrations (>1 month) between the beginning of 1995 and the end of 1998. Respondents were asked about their migration experience and their household food situation in North Korea; they also were measured for Middle Upper-Arm Circumference (MUAC). Data were entered and analyzed with SPSS 8.0. Institutional review boards at Johns Hopkins School of Public Health and in Yanbian Korean Autonomous Prefecture approved the study.

STUDY RESULTS

Mortality, Fertility, and Migration Rates

Between July and September 1999, a total of 381 North Korean migrants were interviewed at 8 sites along the China/DPRK border. Overall, in the 381 households of migrant respondents interviewed in 1999, household size averaged 4.0 persons at the beginning of 1995 and declined to 3.4 persons by the end of 1998. According to 1993 census data released by the DPRK Bureau of Statistics, North Korean households averaged 4.2 members at the end of 1993 and 4.1 in North Hamkyong province where most of our sample originated (Democratic People's Republic of Korea Central Bureau for Statistics, 1997). The average age of people living in the sample households was 30.1 years. The estimated mean age of the North Korean population at the end of 1993 was 27 years. The age structure of the sample population differed from the national population in that 0-9 year olds comprised 19.3 percent of the national population but only 14.6 percent of the sample population and persons aged 60 and over comprised 9.2 percent of the national population compared to 3.7 percent of the sample population. Roughly 57 percent of the sample population were between the ages of 20-59, compared to 44.4 percent in the national population.

Household Mortality

In terms of crude mortality, we observed a death rate of 37.3 per 1,000 averaged over the four-year period, 1995-1998 (see Table 3-1). Standardizing this rate on the age distribution of the 1993 census population would raise it to 41.8 per 1,000.

Figure 3-1 shows age-specific death rates for the sample population, using a four-year average of death rates during the period, 1995-1998. For comparative purposes, we have included the age-specific death rates (ASDRs) from the 1993 census of the DPRK population, which indicated a crude mortality rate of 5.6 per 1000 in 1993. Life expectancy in North Korea was estimated at 66 for males and 73 for females in 1991 (Savada, 1994). We have also included the ASDRs from a model life table, specifically "West" Level 4, which reflects a life expectancy of 25.3 for males and 27.5 for females (Coale and Demeny, 1983). The life expectancy of the sample population was 27.4. Crude mortality among males was 41.1/1000 during the four-year period, compared to 33.8/1000 for females.

TABLE 3-1   Crude Death Rates in Respondent Households (n=381)

Year	Number of Deaths	Midyear Population	Death Rate (per 1,000)
1995	33	1,496	22.1
1996	74	1,429	51.8
1997	68	1,363	49.9
1998	35	1,296	27.0
4-Year Average	210	1,407 (end 1996)	37.3

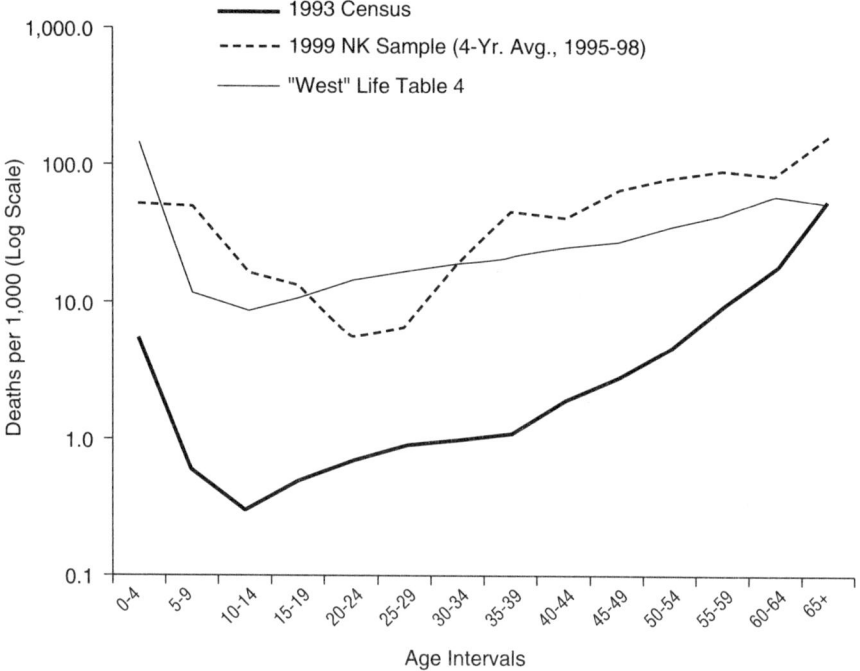

FIGURE 3-1   Age-specific death rates: 1993 Census of North Korea, 1999 sample and "West" Life Table Level 4. Source: Democratic People's Republic of Korea Central Bureau for Statistics (1997); Coale and Demeny (1983).

Overall, crude mortality rates in the 381 North Korean households included in our sample rose from 22.1/1000 in 1995 to 51.8/1000 in 1996 and 49.9/1000 in 1997. The death rate in 1998, however, declined to 27.0/1000. This does not show a return to baseline rates of 5.6/1000 in 1993, but it does suggest that the situation may be improving with stronger harvests and sustained international food aid. It is also possible that mortality is falling because many of the more vulnerable members of the population died off in 1996 and 1997 and the survivors are a hardier group.

We also asked respondents to identify cause of death. Out of 208 who listed a cause of death, 95 deaths (45.7 percent) were attributed to lack of food/malnutrition, and 89 deaths (42.8 percent) were attributed to illness/disease. Accidents were the cause of 12 deaths (5.8 percent) and suicide accounted for 6 deaths (2.9 percent).

TABLE 3-2   Crude Birth Rates in Respondent Households (n=381)

Year	Number of Births	Midyear Population	Birth Rate (per 1,000)
1995	20	1,496	13.4
1996	23	1,429	16.1
1997	22	1,363	16.1
1998	13	1,296	10.0
4-Year Average	78	1,407 (end 1996)	13.9

Household Fertility

Looking at household births during the four-year period, no clear trends emerge except perhaps that fertility in 1998 declined significantly from previous years and that the four-year average, 13.9/1000, is well below the UN estimate of 21.8/1000 for 1990 to 1995 (See Table 3-2).

In- and Out-Migration

Respondents were asked to identify anyone who had moved into or out of the household for more than one month during the four-year recall period. While it is clear from Table 3-3 that net migration rates rose substantially from 1995 to 1997, the data also suggest that cumulative movements in and out of households may have declined from 1997 to 1998. While the net-migration rates for these two years are quite similar, a total of 72 people moved into or out of these households in 1997, while only 50 people did so in 1998.

TABLE 3-3   Net Migration Rates in Respondent Households (n=381)

Year	Number of In-Migrants (>1 Month)	Number of Out-Migrants (>1 Month)	Net Migration	Midyear Population	Net-Migration Rate (per 1,000)
1995	4	10	6	1,496	4.0
1996	5	30	25	1,429	17.5
1997	17	55	38	1,363	27.9
1998	7	43	36	1,296	27.8
Total	33	138	105	1,407 (end 1996)	18.7

TABLE 3-4   Province and Household Mortality

| | Household Mortality, 1995-1998 | | |
Province	No	Yes	Total
North Hamkyong	159	120	279
South Hamkyong	25	15	40
Ryanggang	17	8	25
Other	32	5	37
Total	233	148	381

P = 0.006

Mortality and Household Characteristics

In the following discussion, our unit of analysis is the household and the dependent variable is dichotomous: 0=no deaths in the household, 1995-1998; 1=any deaths in the household, 1995-1998. The 210 deaths reported during the interval occurred in 148 out of 381 households (38.8 percent) in the sample. Except where indicated, we used a chi-square test for significance.

Provincial Address

As shown in Table 3-4, among the 1999 sample, the household address of a large majority (73.2 percent) was in North Hamkyong with South Hamkyong (10.5 percent) a distant second, followed by Ryanggang with 6.6 percent. Only a handful came from other, more distant provinces. Cross-tabulating province of origin with household mortality, we found not only that the association had clear statistical significance (p=0.006), but that the proportion of households with mortality declined with distance of household residence from the China/North Korea border. We had expected to see something of the opposite trend, namely that selectivity for distress as measured by household mortality would be stronger the greater the distance traveled. It is possible, of course, that differential household mortality in the provinces does not reflect migrant selectivity but rather reflects different underlying mortality rates within the provinces.

Residential Area

Just under half (48.8 percent) of respondents described their residential area as urban, while 31.2 percent came from rural/agricultural areas and 20 percent came from mining communities. The mining industry has suffered a virtual shutdown in the northeast, according to many reports, and workers are no longer getting paid. In many of the bigger cities in North and South Hamkyong, reports from migrants suggest that food is no longer available regularly through the government rationing program known as the Public Distribution System (PDS). As one 52-year-old man said, "There are some places that are comparatively better than other places. Along the seacoast, you can catch fish. The steel factories have something to trade with other countries so those workers still are getting paid. Pyongyang is the capital so most of those people get rice. In most big cities, however, the situation is the worst because there is no place to forage or to grow anything." Contrary to expectation, household mortality among migrants coming from urban areas did not differ significantly from that for other areas. Again, it is not possible to tell whether this reflects a more general reality or migration selection.

Family Class Background

All families in North Korea are categorized based on their class background and/or personal characteristics. The ten categories we employed in our study range from worst to best in terms of political standing. The five bad categories include political prisoners and their families, those who collaborated with the Japanese or other enemies of the state, those whose family members went south (into the Republic of Korea), those who have been sent into internal exile, and the families of former rich peasants. All of these categories are grouped into the "hostile" classes in terms of political orientation (Asia Watch and Minnesota Lawyers International Human Rights Committee, 1988). The middle peasant and poor peasant categories are largely neutral although poor peasant status is helpful in obtaining membership in the Korean Workers Party. Three categories comprise the "loyal" classes: families of war victims, veterans, and revolutionary heroes. It is interesting to note that from 1995 to 1998, the political standing among these migrant households went categorically downward (see Table 3-5). The number of households with a "hostile" class designation increased by nearly 60 percent, from 29 to 46, during the four years. What this suggests, among other things, is that declining political status may provide a strong incentive to leave North Korea.

Running a cross-tabulation of household mortality by political class, we found no significant association, which suggests either that recent mortality is not correlated with a household's political status or that, among the "loyal" class categories, migration to China may be more selective for higher mortality.

TABLE 3-5   Family Class Background of North Korean Households (n=380)

Category 1995	Number in 1995	Percent in 1995	Number in 1998	Percent in 1998
"Hostile" Class	29	7.6	46	12.1
"Wavering" Class	285	75.2	284	74.7
"Loyal" Class	65	17.2	50	13.2
Total	379	100.0	380	100.0

Source of Food

Historically, nearly three-quarters of the North Korean population have been entitled to purchase heavily subsidized food rations through the government's Public Distribution System (PDS). Under this 10-tiered structure based on age and occupational status, a working adult was entitled to 700 grams of food-grain per day, with children receiving 500 grams and the elderly 600 grams per day. By 1997, according to UN estimates, PDS allocations were averaging only about 100 grams per person per day (World Food Programme, 1997). Respondents in the 1999 survey reported that their per capita daily food ration was 81 grams in 1997. As Table 3-6 indicates, while a majority of respondents (50.7 percent) relied on government rations as their household's primary source of food in 1995, by 1997 only 3.9 percent did so. Instead, nearly 44 percent of

TABLE 3-6   Household's Primary Source of Food by Year, Total Number of Respondents (Percentage of Total Number of Respondents)

Year	Govt. Ration	Buy	Barter	Forage	Gift	Grow	Other	Total
1995	193 (50.7%)	44 (11.5)	46 (12.1)	55 (14.4)	2 (0.5)	35 (9.2)	6 (1.6)	381 (100.0)
1996	82 (21.5)	62 (16.3)	58 (15.2)	113 (29.7)	2 (0.5)	57 (15.0)	7 (1.8)	381 (100.0)
1997	15 (3.9)	43 (11.3)	83 (21.8)	166 (43.6)	5 (1.3)	61 (16.0)	8 (2.1)	381 (100.0)
1998	30 (7.9)	40 (10.5)	72 (18.9)	167 (43.8)	4 (1.0)	58 (15.2)	10 (2.6)	381 (100.0)

TABLE 3-7   Primary Food Source (1998) and
Household Mortality

| | Household Mortality, 1995-1998 | | |
Food Source	No	Yes	Total
Govt. Ration	19	11	30
Buy	28	12	40
Barter	56	16	72
Forage	79	88	167
Gift	4	0	4
Grow	40	18	58
Other	7	3	10
Total	232	147	379

P = 0.000

households in 1997 and 1998 relied on foraging as their principal source of food. A slight improvement in the situation might be seen in the increased percentage of households relying on government rations in 1998 (7.9 percent) compared to 3.9 percent during the previous year.

As Table 3-7 indicates, fully 60 percent of all households reporting mortality from 1995-1998 relied on foraging as their primary source of food for at least two years. Of the 167 households who primarily foraged for their food supply in 1998 (and in 1997 as well), 88 of 167 (53 percent) reported at least one death in the household, a proportion substantially higher than those households relying on any other food source. We are not necessarily suggesting a direct causal relationship between foraging and household mortality, but the association is clearly a strong one.

Mortality and Migrant Characteristics

The mean age of respondents was 33.3 and nearly 80 percent were under the age of 40. More than 95 percent had completed at least a middle-school education and nearly 45 percent had completed at least a high-school education. Factory workers comprised the single most common occupation (40.6 percent), followed by farmers (19.5 percent) and unemployed (9.8 percent). More than 55 percent of the 1999 survey respondents said that their principal reason for coming to China was to get food, while another 36 percent said they wanted to work or make money. More than 80 percent were visiting China for the first time since 1995. Of those who had come previously, the average length of stay was 52 days, although the great majority (60 percent) stayed less than one month. Respondents reported that they had traveled an average of 143 kilometers from their home to the border and another 127 kilometers from the border to the site where they were interviewed. The second figure, if accurate, reflects a significant amount of local movement within China. It is probably not a measurement "as the crow flies" from the border to the site. Asked if they planned to return to North Korea, 56 percent responded yes.

Sex

Among the 1999 sample, 53 percent of respondents were male and 47 percent were female. As Table 3-8 demonstrates, 44 percent of households represented by a male migrant respondent in China had at least one death during 1995-1998 while 33 percent of households represented by a female migrant experienced a death in the recall period. This difference, which is statistically significant ($p=0.027$), cannot be explained by the fact that overall male mortality rates within migrant households (39.6/1000) was higher than female mortality rates (34.9/1000). In fact, males reported only slightly higher death rates for males in their households (41.1/1000) than female respondents reported for males in their households (37.5/1000). The real difference was in female mortality, with male respondents reporting much higher female mortality (47.5/1000) in their households than female respondents reported (18.1/1000) in theirs.

Marital Status

While household mortality does seem to be associated with marital status ($p=0.002$), it should be noted that the difference between married and single persons appears negligible (see Table 3-9). Divorced and widowed persons, however, have a much greater likelihood of household

TABLE 3-8   Sex of Respondent and Household Mortality

	Household Mortality, 1995-1998		
Sex	No	Yes	Total
Male	113	89	202
Female	120	59	179
Total	233	148	381

P = 0.027

TABLE 3-9   Marital Status of Respondent and
Household Mortality

| | Household Mortality, 1995-1998 | | |
Marital Status	No	Yes	Total
Married	115	67	182
Single	100	53	153
Divorced	3	12	15
Widowed	5	13	18
Separated	9	3	12
Total	232	148	380

P = 0.002

mortality (widows were already widowed as of January 1995 and all mortality was subsequent to that).

Disaggregating for gender of respondents, however, we find that while household mortality did not differ between male and female *married* respondents, significant differences existed between male and female *single* respondents. Among single male respondents, deaths were reported in 50 percent of all households (35 of 70) while among single female respondents, deaths in the recall period were reported in only 22 percent (18 of 83) of households. Another difference we found when disaggregating for gender of respondents is that all of the mortality in households of *divorced* respondents occurred in households of male respondents; no divorced females were even present in the survey. Conversely, all of the mortality in households of *widowed* respondents occurred in households of female respondents; only one widowed male was present in the survey and he reported no deaths in his household from 1995-1998.

Middle-Upper Arm Circumference (MUAC)

Respondents in the 1998 survey were measured for middle upper-arm circumference as a rough measure of adult nutritional status. We employed a cut-point of less than 200 millimeters for males and less than 190 millimeters for females as an indicator of Grade 4 malnutrition or severe wasting and less than 230 millimeters for males and less than 220 millimeters for females as an indicator of undernourishment (Ferro-Luzzi and James, 1996). Adjusting for rounding, we found that 5.2 percent (10/194) of male respondents were severely wasted and 28.9 percent (56/194) were undernourished. Among females, 3.4 percent (5/146) were severely wasted and 32.8 percent (48/146) were undernourished. Total MUAC scores ranged from a low of 165 millimeters (female) to a high of 298 millimeters (2 males). Running a logistic regression of all MUAC scores on household mortality, we found a slight negative correlation with no statistical significance (p=0.134). Disaggregating for gender, however, we found that among male migrant respondents, MUAC scores had a strong negative correlation with household mortality (p=0.009) while among female respondents, there was no such correlation (p=0.676).

ANALYSIS AND CONCLUSIONS

The crude death rates among the North Korean households that include a migrant to China reflect a pattern of mortality that is well in excess of normal and that climaxes in the years 1996 and 1997, when most accounts suggest that the famine was at its peak. Although we have no way of measuring the extent to which these rates reflect a broader reality, we did undertake to assess death rates among households that did not include a migrant to China. We did this by asking the migrant respondent to describe the separate household of a sibling and then asking if anyone in that sibling household had visited China during the recall period. Out of 381 migrants interviewed, 142 provided basic demographic information on a sibling, nonmigrant household. Within these sibling households, mortality rates during 1995-1998 averaged 59.1/1000, with rates peaking in 1996 and 1997 and then declining in 1998. Although we stress that this is not an independent sample, these data suggest that elevated mortality may affect more than those households that have sent a migrant into China.

In addition to excess mortality, the sample of North Korean households demonstrates two other trends that are consistent with a response to famine: declining fertility and rising levels of migration. The drop in birth rates in 1998 would suggest that many families began to control their fertility in 1997, allowing a nine-month lag for gestation. As noted earlier, the migration patterns (which largely are measures of internal, not international, migration) also support the view that more people were moving in and out of households when the famine was at its peak in 1997.

The survey found three ways in which household food security was associated with mortality in migrant households. First, the highest proportion of households experiencing at least one death in the recall period was found among those that had relied on foraging as their primary source of food for at least two years. Second, more than 45 percent of all deaths reported by migrant respondents were attributed to malnutrition or insufficient food. Third, among male migrant respondents at least, middle upper arm circumference was negatively associated (p=0.009) with household mortality. The fact that no such association existed with female respondents suggests either some physiological cause or, perhaps more likely, that male and female migrants may differ from one another in the extent to which food insecurity and household mortality motivate their movements into, and back from, China.

As we have tried to suggest throughout this paper, without solid data on recent household mortality in North Korea, it is next to impossible to know if a correlation observed in the migrant household sample is representative of a broader trend or merely indicative of a selection factor for migration. Looking at mortality differentials within the sample, however, it is possible to conclude that male and female migrants may be playing somewhat different roles in terms of household coping strategies. As noted earlier, male migrants are associated with higher proportions of households with mortality than female migrants (44 percent compared to 33 percent, p=0.027). A higher percentage of males than females have visited China more than once since 1995 (22 percent compared to 15.3 percent, p=0.064), and more males than females report having relatives in China (20.1 percent compared to 11.8 percent, p=0.029). Males also have a greater likelihood of returning to North Korea than females (65.8 percent compared to 44.9 percent, p<0.001).

One difference between male and female migrants that may help to explain these patterns is that female migrants are more likely than males to be single (46.6 percent compared to 34.6 percent, p=0.018) or widowed (9.5 percent to 0.5 percent, p<0.001). Although male and female migrants do not differ significantly in age or household size, the difference in marital status may partly explain why married and divorced males appear more likely to respond to distress in the household by going into China and returning with food or other assistance. Single or widowed females, on the other hand, may be more likely to respond to distress by leaving the household, thus reducing the number of mouths left to feed. Particularly for single North Korean females, the prospects for remaining more permanently in China are enhanced by the active "bride-trade" along the border.

When using small, selective samples to estimate the dimensions of a possibly much larger phenomenon, the limitations are obvious. Surveys of migrant populations cannot take the place of random sample surveys in the population at large, especially if one is interested in estimating national trends in mortality, fertility, or migration. Refugee and migrant surveys, however, may be necessary in situations of political or military crisis, natural disaster, severe government restrictions, or any combination of the above, if that is the only way of deriving needed indicators for an otherwise inaccessible population.

In the case of North Korea, the findings from our survey have several implications for the humanitarian community. First, our sample provides evidence of significantly elevated mortality among at least some North Korean households, especially in North Hamkyong province. This excess mortality, moreover, was associated with food insecurity. The age-specific death rates in our sample population indicated that excess mortality was found not only in the youngest and oldest segments of the population—although these showed the highest absolute increases—but also among older children and younger to middle-aged adults. The consolidated UN inter-agency appeal for the DPRK in 2000 targeted 8,044,000 beneficiaries, 75 percent of whom were children and another 5 percent of whom were elderly (aged 60 and above) (United Nations Office for the Coordination of Humanitarian Affairs, 1999). Nearly two-thirds (63 percent) of all deaths reported in our survey, however, occurred to people between the ages of 20 and 59, suggesting that not all high-risk groups will benefit from UN-supported feeding programs. A majority of beneficiaries, moreover, are targeted through government institutions (kindergartens, primary and secondary schools, orphanages, hospitals, factories, and collective farms). Children who are not in school, adults who are unemployed, and people of any age who are away from their registered residence or place of work are unlikely to be reached either by UN or government-sponsored food distributions.

Migrant surveys are important for their own sake, even when migrants do not represent the broader picture. First, simply because they exist, forced migrants may be signals of crisis and distress that otherwise might be hidden from the international community. Second, forced migrants—both international and internal—may be among the most vulnerable populations in any complex humanitarian emergency. And third, questions and issues that emerge from these surveys may help to shape a broader response to crisis. International refugees and migrants too often are treated as a separate and distinct problem from the crisis they have supposedly left behind. Migrant surveys may help us see not only that these problems are of a piece but also how better to solve them in a more comprehensive manner.

ACKNOWLEDGMENTS

Support for this study came from the Center of Excellence in Disaster Management and Humanitarian Assistance and the Andrew W. Mellon Foundation. Fieldwork was carried out in collaboration with Mercy Corps International.

REFERENCES

Asia Watch and Minnesota Lawyers International Human Rights Committee
1988 *Human Rights in the Democratic People's Republic of Korea (North Korea)*. Minneapolis and Washington, D.C.: Asia Watch and Minnesota Lawyers International Human Rights Committee.

Coale, A.J., and P. Demeny
1983 *Regional Model Life Tables and Stable Populations*. New York: Academic Press.

Democratic People's Republic of Korea Central Bureau for Statistics
1997 *Population by Location and Households, December 31, 1993*. World Food Programme Mimeograph.

Eberstadt, N., and J. Banister
1992 *The Population of North Korea*. Berkeley: University of California, Institute of East Asian Studies.

European Union, United Nations Children's Fund, and World Food Programme
1998 *Nutrition Survey of the Democratic People's Republic of Korea*. New York: UNICEF.

Ferro-Luzzi, A., and W. James
1996 Adult malnutrition: Simple assessment techniques for use in emergencies. *British Journal of Nutrition* 753:10.

Katona-Apte, J., and A. Mokdad
1998 Malnutrition of children in the Democratic People's Republic of North Korea. *Journal of Nutrition* 128(8):1315-1319.

Korean Buddhist Sharing Movement
1998 *The Food Crisis of North Korea Witnessed by 1,019 Food Refugees*. Seoul: Korean Buddhist Sharing Movement.

Robinson, W.C., M. Lee, K. Hill, and G. Burnham
1999 Mortality in North Korean migrant households. *Lancet* 3542:91-95.

Savada, A.M.
1994 *North Korea: A Country Study*. Washington, D.C.: Federal Research Division, Library of Congress.

United Nations Department of Economic and Social Affairs
1998 *1996 Demographic Yearbook*. New York: United Nations, Department of Economic and Social Affairs.

United Nations Office for the Coordination of Humanitarian Affairs
1999 *UN Consolidated Interagency Appeal for Democratic People's Republic of Korea, January-December 2000*. Geneva: United Nations.

World Food Programme
1997 *On the Knife Edge of a Famine*. Rome: World Food Programme.

World Vision
1997 *North Korea Food Questionnaire*. Federal Way, Washington: World Vision.

4

Methods of Determining Mortality in the Mass Displacement and Return of Emergency-Affected Populations in Kosovo, 1998-1999

Brent Burkholder, Paul Spiegel, and Peter Salama

INTRODUCTION

In early 1998, long-standing tensions between the majority ethnic Albanian and minority Serbian populations in the Federal Republic of Yugoslavia (FRY) province of Kosovo broke out into open hostilities. Fighting intensified throughout the year between an armed resistance movement, the Kosovo Liberation Army (KLA), and local Serbian police and military forces, resulting in the destruction of multiple towns and the internal displacement of thousands of ethnic Albanians. Following the failure of diplomatic initiatives in early 1999, the North Atlantic Treaty Organization (NATO) began an organized bombing campaign in Kosovo on March 24, 1999. During the subsequent three months, additional ethnic violence forced almost 70 percent of the estimated 1.9 million Kosovar Albanians to leave their homes. Approximately 500,000 remained displaced within Kosovo and another 775,000 fled as refugees, including 444,600 to Albania, 244,500 to the Former Yugoslav Republic of Macedonia (FYROM), and 69,900 to the province of Montenegro (see Figure 4-1) (del Mundo and Wilkinson, 1999). After the signing of a peace accord on June 10, 1999, the flood of refugees reversed, and within three weeks more than 600,000 people had returned to Kosovo, one of the fastest repatriations in modern times (del Mundo and Wilkinson, 1999).

Tracking the mortality associated with the violence, movements, and conditions of displacement suffered by the emergency-affected populations during this crisis proved extremely problematic. During the height

FIGURE 4-1　Map of Kosovo region, June 15, 1999.　Source: United States Agency for International Development (1999).

of the violence from March to June 1999 there were no outside observers in Kosovo. Even within Albania and FYROM, the wide dispersal of the refugees into multiple small collective centers and host families limited access to large portions of this population. United Nations (UN) agencies and nongovernmental organizations (NGOs) did establish emergency surveillance systems in these two countries. However, logistical problems and the challenges of integrating these emergency operations into local, ongoing surveillance systems led to difficulties in obtaining comprehensive health data.

Nevertheless, it is important to provide a record of mortality associated with this crisis and to highlight the challenges of collecting and analyzing data that confronted epidemiologists in the field. Our best estimates are that the absolute levels of mortality among the Kosovar refugees were not elevated as compared to previous complex emergencies. However, in addition to providing mortality results, we will focus on the methods required to both obtain and analyze this mortality data through surveillance systems in Albania and FYROM, as well as through a retrospective survey in Kosovo itself. In both scenarios, obtaining accurate population figures for denominator data or sample frame determination proved as problematic as obtaining information on deaths.

For information on Albania and FYROM, Burkholder collected information from a variety of sources, principally from surveillance systems operational during the crisis. In Kosovo, Spiegel and Salama conducted a retrospective population-based health survey between September 8 and September 17, 1999. The survey was a collaborative effort between the International Rescue Committee (IRC), the Kosovo Institute of Public Health (IPH), the World Health Organization (WHO), and the Centers for Disease Control and Prevention (CDC).

METHODS

Albania and FYROM Surveillance Systems in Kosovar Refugee Camps

Denominators: Obtaining Population Estimates

The United Nations High Commissioner for Refugees (UNHCR) had comparatively complete figures for the relatively small number of Kosovar Albanians who fled into neighboring countries prior to the NATO bombing on March 24, 1999. However, from that point until the second week of April, refugee population estimates in both Albania and FYROM varied widely due to the chaotic influx of large masses of refugees crossing the borders daily. UNHCR was gradually able to begin a more systematic enumeration process in cooperation with local governments, the International Organization for Migration (IOM), and the local Red Cross societies. By March 27 in Albania, and April 15 in FYROM, UNHCR issued daily reports on the number of new refugees and estimates of total refugees residing in the host country.[1] We obtained detailed population demographic information for camp refugees in FYROM from the IOM registration data bank (International Organization for Migration, 1999).

Mortality Surveillance

In Albania, the government's Institute of Public Health, UN agencies, and NGOs collaborated on the Kosovar Refugee Information System (KRYSIS) which began collecting health data on a weekly basis beginning on April 16 (Instituti Shendetit Publik and World Health Organization, 1999; Ministry of Health of the Republic of Albania et al., 1999). The system attempted to incorporate reporting from local government health clinics in all 37 districts as well as from health posts established by NGOs in refugee camps. While timeliness and completeness varied from week to week, over 86 percent of all health units participated (Instituti Shendetit Publik and World Health Organization, 1999; Valenciano et al., 1999). Because an Epicentre rapid assessment in Kukes (Perea, 1999) and other reports early in the emergency found relatively low mortality rates, the surveillance system purposely focused on outpatient facilities and targeted communicable diseases (Coulombier, 1999). Although KRYSIS did report some deaths which occurred in camps or local clinics, most mortality was tracked through a hospital surveillance system which reported directly to the Ministry of Health (Albanian Ministry of Health Statistic Unit, 1999). Line listings of deaths were not available; however, there does not appear to be duplication between these two sources (Coulombier, 1999). Age and cause of death were provided only for reports from the KRYSIS. Due to the limitations listed above, refugee deaths that occurred in Albania are most likely under-reported to a greater extent than in FYROM.

In FYROM, we obtained information on deaths that occurred in the camps during the early phase of the crisis through personal communication with field hospital staff (Alkan, 1999; Beckman, 1999). Later, deaths were reported through the Macedonian Refugee Communicable Disease Surveillance System, which began weekly standardized data collection from NGO camp health posts and field hospitals on April 26, 1999 (World Health Organization Regional Office for Europe et al., 1999). The Ministry of the Interior (MOI) provided an additional list of all refugee deaths that occurred in state hospitals between mid-March and June 30, 1999 (Former Yugoslav Republic of Macedonia Ministry of the Interior, 1999).

---

[1] Additional population figures were obtained from daily refugee population reports produced by UNHCR in Tirana, Albania, and Skopje, FYROM.

Although deaths occurring in the camps were also required to have FYROM official death certificates, a careful comparison of both camp and MOI lists did not reveal any duplications. Additional deaths were discovered through a listing of funerals provided by a local Albanian NGO (El Hillal, 1999).

Kosovo Retrospective Mortality Survey[2]

To assess mortality rates, major causes of death and the risk factors for mortality during the civil war period of February 1998 to June 1999, we conducted a two-stage cluster survey in the 25 predominantly Albanian municipalities of Kosovo. Assuming a doubling of the baseline mortality rate and a design effect of 4, we calculated a total sample population of 6,440 individuals or 1,200 households.

We chose villages or city neighborhoods as our sampling unit; however, determining a proper population sampling frame proved extremely difficult due to the lack of current demographic information. The most recent census data from 1991 was outdated by the crisis-induced population displacement over the last year. Nevertheless, we took this census as the best available baseline and updated the figures for each village and/or neighborhood based upon population estimates made after July 1999 by UNHCR, the NATO intervention Kosovo force (KFOR), and food distribution lists from various NGOs. The sample was stratified to account for rural/urban and destroyed/non-destroyed status and 50 clusters (of 24 households each) were then assigned based on probability proportional to size. Households within each cluster were selected according to the standard method used by the Expanded Program on Immunization. One member of each household was interviewed and asked to provide a household census during the month of January 1998 and to recount information on the whereabouts of each individual, including any deaths that had occurred since that time.

RESULTS

Population Estimations: Kosovar Refugees in Albania and FYROM

From 1998 through mid-March 1999, approximately 25,000 refugees crossed into Albania fleeing the ethnic violence in Kosovo. In the two

---

[2] Detailed information on survey methodology and results can be found in Spiegel and Salama (2000). This survey includes deaths among all Albanian Kosovars: refugees, internally displaced, and those who never left their homes.

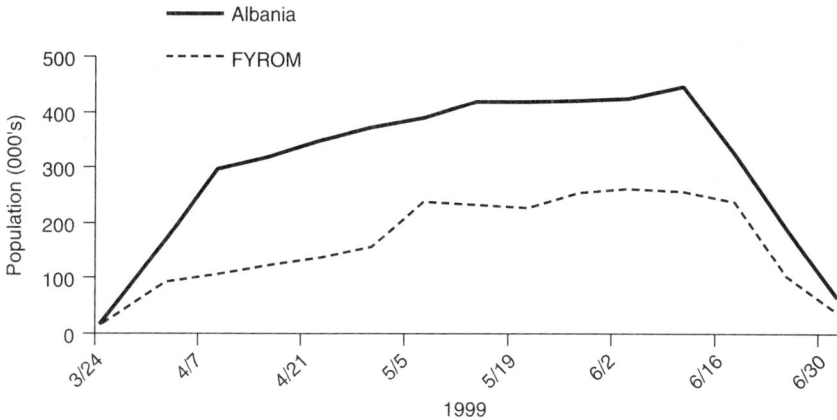

FIGURE 4-2   Number of Kosovar refugees in Albania and the Former Yugoslav Republic of Macedonia (FYROM), March 24-June 30, 1999.

weeks following the NATO bombing on March 24, 1999, an estimated 285,000 refugees entered the Kukes region of northern Albania. A slow, steady stream of additional refugees followed. The refugee population in Albania peaked in mid-June 1999 at a total of 444,500 (see Figure 4-2) (del Mundo and Wilkinson, 1999; United States Agency for International Development, 1999). Refugees were eventually dispersed throughout the country. Over two-thirds lived with host families, another 20 percent were housed in 22 camps, and the remainder were accommodated in multiple small collective centers (United States Agency for International Development, 1999). Repatriation occurred almost as quickly as the initial influx. Between June 15 and June 30, 1999, over 287,000 refugees returned home to Kosovo and the vast majority of those remaining returned within the next month.[3]

Population flows into FYROM were slightly smaller in terms of numbers, but no less dramatic. Only 16,000 refugees had crossed the border before the NATO bombing, but in the subsequent two weeks another 101,000 Kosovar Albanians fled into FYROM. Over the next months, further immigration varied considerably depending on the level of violence in Kosovo and the ease of border crossing. Eventually, by June 15, 1999, over 245,000 refugees would reach the FYROM (World Health Organization Regional Office for Europe et al., 1999). At that time, 43 per-

---

[3] Additional population figures were obtained from daily refugee population reports produced by UNHCR in Tirana, Albania and Skopje, FYROM.

cent were living in 8 refugee camps and the remainder were housed with host families, primarily in the 5 regions near the border (Former Yugoslav Republic of Macedonia Ministry of the Interior, 1999). Almost 202,000 returned home by the end of June.

Population fluctuations in FYROM were even more pronounced because of the UNHCR/IOM Humanitarian Evacuation Program. Between April 5 and June 25, 1999, 90,189 refugees in the FYROM were evacuated to third countries.[4] This movement led to huge population shifts, particularly in the two camps that were the primary source of evacuees. For example, during the last three weeks in May, 44,417 refugees left the Macedonian camps and 46,492 arrived.

Demographic data are available only for the refugee camp population in FYROM. According to IOM registration data on May 27, 1999, the age-gender distribution of the camp population was roughly similar to that of the Kosovar population found in the 1991 census (International Organization for Migration, 1999).

MORTALITY

Crude Mortality Rates

Table 4-1 shows reported deaths and crude mortality rates (CMRs) from both surveillance systems in refugee camps in Albania and FYROM, and the retrospective survey. Of the 141 refugee deaths reported in Albania, the KRYSIS (Ministry of Health of the Republic of Albania et al., 1999) reported 34 and the Ministry of Health (Albanian Ministry of Health Statistic Unit, 1999) reported 107 from hospital surveillance. In FYROM, the camp surveillance system (World Health Organization Regional Office for Europe et al., 1999) detected 28 (16 percent) refugee deaths and the Ministry of Interior (Former Yugoslav Republic of Macedonia Ministry of the Interior, 1999) reported 143 (76 percent). Field hospital directors were aware of five additional deaths in the first week of the refugee influx in early April. The NGO funeral list (El Hillal, 1999) included 34 deaths, of which 11 were not found in any other sources.

There was a difference in the Albanian and FYROM refugee CMRs (0.11 versus 0.14 and 0.24 versus 0.33, respectively), based on whether the midpoint or average population was used to calculate the denominator. However, the difference was not statistically significant in either case (z-statistic to compare rates).

---

[4] Again, additional population figures were obtained from daily refugee population reports produced by UNHCR in Tirana, Albania and Skopje, FYROM.

TABLE 4-1 Crude Mortality Rates (CMRs) in Kosovo, February 1998-June 1999, and among Kosovar Refugees in Albania and the Former Yugoslav Republic of Macedonia (FYROM), March-June 1999

	Time Period	Reported Deaths	Midpoint Population	CMR (Deaths/1,000/Month)	Average Population	CMR (Deaths/1,000/Month)
Kosovo Baseline	1996	N/A	N/A	N/A	N/A	0.31
Refugees in FYROM	3/20/99–6/30/99	187	232,900	0.24	170,063	0.33
Refugees in Albania[a]	4/1/99–6/30/99	141	432,267	0.11	334,778	0.14
Kosovo Survey[b]	2/1/98–6/30/99				Initial Population	
All causes		105	N/A	N/A	8,553	0.72
War-related		67	N/A	N/A	8,553	0.46

Sources: Ministry of Health of the Republic of Albania et al. (1999); Albanian Ministry of Health Statistic Unit (1999); World Health Organization Regional Office for Europe et al. (1999); Former Yugoslav Republic of Macedonia Ministry of the Interior (1999); and El Hillal (1999). [a]There was significant underreporting of Kosovo refugee deaths in Albania. [b]Displaced and nondisplaced.

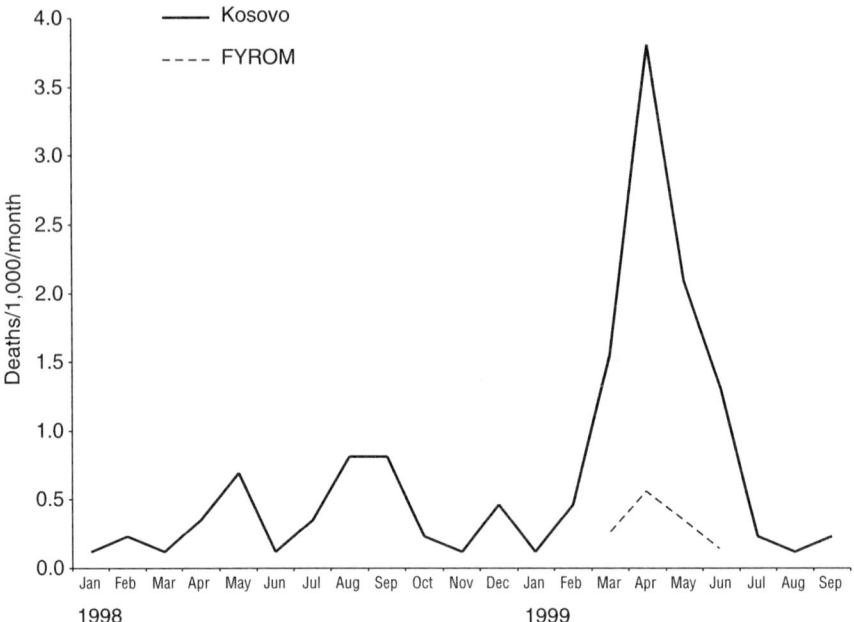

FIGURE 4-3   Crude mortality rate in Kosovo, January 1998-September 1999, and among Kosovar refugees in the Former Yugoslav Republic of Macedonia (FYROM), March-June 1999.

The retrospective mortality survey in Kosovo that covered the complete 17-month period of the crisis found a much higher overall CMR (0.72 per 1,000 per month). Note that the data sources for the surveillance and the retrospective survey are not mutually exclusive. The respondents to the survey in Kosovo included refugees who had returned from FYROM (as well as other countries) and therefore may be reporting deaths that were also included in the surveillance system.

Figure 4-3 shows that mortality during the Kosovo crisis peaked in April 1999. In FYROM, the death rate in the refugee camps was highest during April in the initial phase of the refugee exodus and then steadily declined. Even during April, the CMR only reached 0.56 per 1,000 per month (6.7 per 1,000 per year) in the refugee camps. The Kosovo data show a similar pattern but with a much higher peak CMR of 3.25 per 1,000 per month (39 per 1,000 per year). This major increase in mortality and smaller peaks throughout 1998 closely correspond to flare-ups in fighting. As stated below, the majority of the elevated mortality was due to war-related trauma.

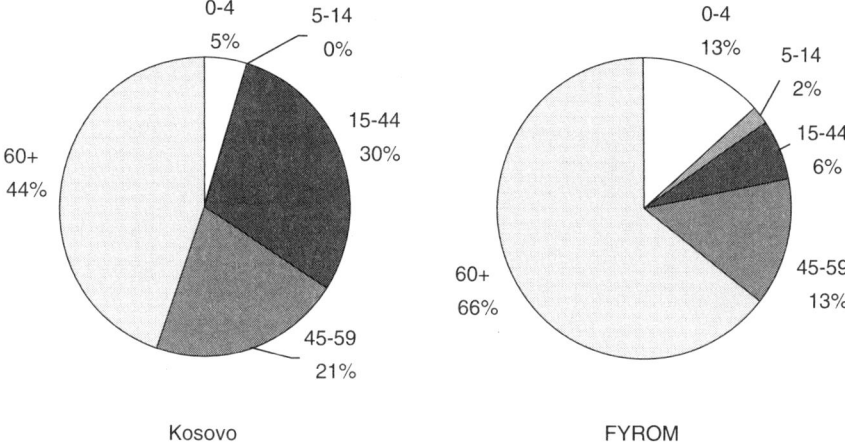

Kosovo   FYROM

FIGURE 4-4   Age-specific mortality of Kosovar Albanians in Kosovo, February 1, 1998-June 30, 1999 (N=105) and in the Former Yugoslav Republic of Macedonia (FYROM), March 20-June 30, 1999 (N=141).

Age, Sex, and Cause-Specific Mortality

Specific information on mortality in Albania was limited (Valenciano et al., 1999). Between April 16 and June 6, 1999, this surveillance system reported 34 deaths; 11 in children under 5 years old and 23 among those over 5 years old.   Cause of death was clearly specified in only 17 cases. Among children under 5 years, death was attributed to acute respiratory infection in 3 (36 percent) cases; and among those over 5 years, 3 (13 percent) were also due to acute respiratory infection and 11 (48 percent) deaths were labeled as "cardiac."

Males accounted for 54 percent of the deaths in FYROM. Specific age data was available for only 141 (75 percent) of the 187 deaths (see Figure 4-4). The majority (66 percent) of deaths were in adults 60 years and over. Of the 19 deaths in children under 5 years, 15 occurred among neonates and were ascribed to either "prematurity" or "aspiration."   Over 55 percent of all deaths were attributed to either "natural causes" or chronic disease (see Figure 4-5). There were few infectious disease deaths. The "other" category included two deaths due to hypothermia, two to gunshots, and one due to a motor vehicle accident. Seventy-one (40 percent) deaths occurred among refugees who lived in camps and 112 (60 percent) occurred among host-family refugees (Ministry of Health of the Republic of Albania et al., 1999). There was no statistical significance in the CMR based on residence status (data not shown).

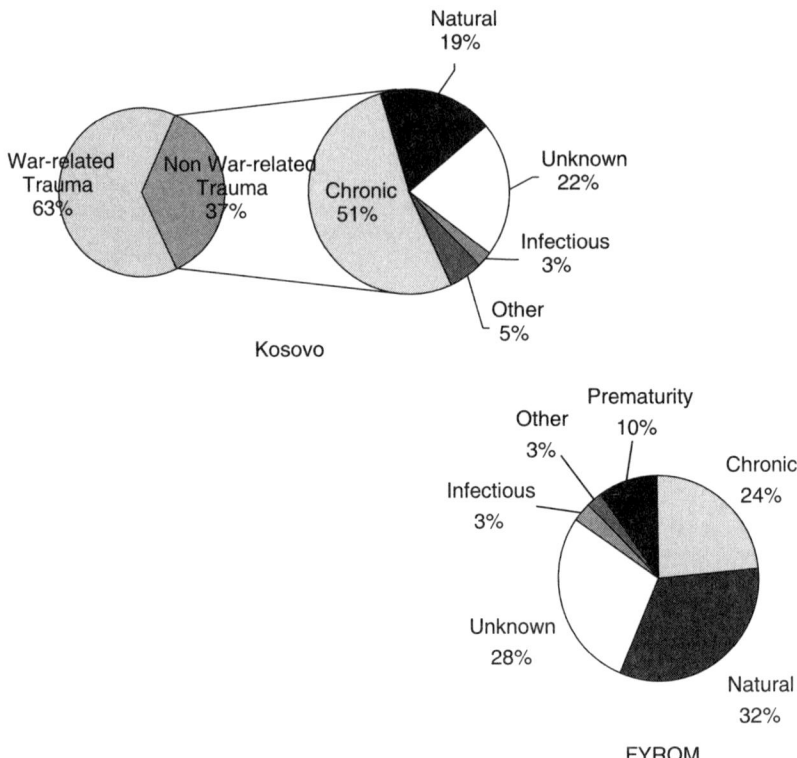

FIGURE 4-5   Proportional mortality of Kosovar Albanians in Kosovo, February 1, 1998-June 30, 1999 (N=105) and in the Former Yugoslav Republic of Macedonia (FYROM), March 20-June 30, 1999 (N=187).

In the Kosovo survey, males accounted for 67 percent of all reported deaths, a higher proportion than in FYROM.   Unlike FYROM, a smaller percentage of deaths occurred among the 60 years and older age group (44 percent), while a much larger proportion occurred among the 15 to 59 year olds (51 percent).   A smaller percentage of deaths under 5 years (5 percent) occurred in the Kosovo survey, possibly due to methodological problems in capturing infant deaths in a retrospective survey (see Figure 4-4).   "War-related trauma," which constituted the largest cause of death (63 percent), was defined as any death occurring directly or as a result of an injury sustained during the conflict (see Figure 4-5).   These war-related traumas included summary and arbitrary killings with bullets, shrapnel or other munitions, or by the burning or collapsing of buildings, bridges, and other structures. In data not shown here, we found that 24 (36 percent) of the 67 deaths due to war-related trauma were among the elderly (60 years and older), and of this group, 92 percent were male. The elderly were 5.9 times (95 percent confidence interval: 3.6-6.6) more likely to die from this cause than any other age group.   Among the non-war-related causes of death, chronic disease and "natural" causes accounted for 70 percent of the deaths. As in FYROM, infectious diseases only accounted for a relatively small percentage of deaths.

LIMITATIONS

Albania and FYROM Surveillance Systems in Kosovar Refugee Camps

The relative lack of mortality data from Albania precludes making any conclusions about the status of refugees in that country or drawing any comparisons to those in FYROM. The wide geographic disbursement of the refugees, their access to multiple health facilities, and the understandable focus of the surveillance system on outpatient clinics seem to have complicated the process of tracking mortality in this setting.

Even in FYROM, where the refugees were more concentrated and had access to only a limited number of health centers and hospitals, it is difficult to gauge accurately the completeness of reporting. Deaths occurring during the early chaos of the influx may not have been reported. After that period, reporting for camp refugees should have been more complete since these refugees were either treated in camp field hospitals or were directly transported to one of a limited number of local tertiary care centers. However, only 28 (39 percent) of 71 camp refugee deaths were reported by the camp surveillance system; the remainder were reported months later through routine channels.   Additionally, due to FYROM government restrictions on travel and access to health facilities, host family refugees may have been less likely to seek care. Underreporting of deaths may be likely among this group, particularly for those in rural areas. The local NGO funeral list was impossible to verify; however 11 of the 34 deaths they reported were not on the official MOI record.

There were similar limitations in obtaining accurate denominator data. The rapid mass movement of the refugees at multiple border crossings, the refugees' wide geographic dispersal, and their distribution into multiple types of accommodations all presented challenges to obtaining accurate estimations of the number of people involved.   Refugees arriving before early April routinely made their own arrangements for housing with host families.   Only refugees who arrived later were sent to camps or, in the case of Albania, to camps or collective centers. Registration in the confines of camps or collective centers was difficult due to the constant influx of new arrivals and, in FYROM, departures for third countries, but nevertheless proved easier than dealing with refugees in host families. Enumeration was particularly delayed in FYROM where host family refugees had to go through a multistage registration process before inclusion on the official Macedonian Red Cross list.

Kosovo Retrospective Mortality Survey

This survey has some of the same limitations that have been pointed out in previous retrospective mortality studies (Ascherio et al., 1992). The 17-month recall period is relatively long and could potentially introduce recall bias. Survivor bias can be present in any such surveys since households in which all members have died or remain refugees could not have been selected. Additionally, limitations related to verbal autopsies can make cause of death determinations problematic.

Epidemiologists in Kosovo had additional constraints, particularly in estimating local population figures for sample determination. Inaccurate or outdated census data and lack of current population figures can introduce selection bias in any conflict situation, but these factors may have introduced particular challenges in this case due to the exceptionally high percent of household displacement. Furthermore, there may be inherent limitations to using cluster sampling for mortality surveys in general.

DISCUSSION

Albania and FYROM Surveillance Systems in Kosovar Refugee Camps

While the validity of the data cannot be confirmed due to the possible exclusion of Kosovar Albanians from the surveillance system, the Kosovo Institute of Public Health reported an average CMR of 4.0 per 1,000 per year (0.33 per 1,000 per month) for 1989-1996 (Kosovo Institute of Public Health, 1997). Compared to this baseline, the CMR available from the KRYSIS and Albanian MOH for refugees in Albania is exceedingly low. These surveillance systems did not concentrate on mortality so the low rates most likely represent underreporting.

The aggregated mortality data on refugees in FYROM appears to be more complete; however, the CMR is still quite low by any comparison to emergency standards. Certainly the mortality rate did not come close to the previously accepted complex emergency threshold of greater than 1 death per 10,000 per day, or 3 per 1,000 per month (Sphere Project Steering Committee for Humanitarian Response and Interaction, 1998). The average CMR for the three-month crisis was markedly similar to the pre-war baseline and surpassed it only during the height of the crisis in April. Even allowing for substantial underreporting, it appears that the Kosovar Albanians were a generally healthy and relatively young population whose health status was maintained during their refuge in the FYROM.

Kosovo Retrospective Mortality Survey

The Kosovo survey did report an average CMR between February 1998 and June 1999 that was 2.3 times higher than the preconflict baseline. However, only during the month of April 1999 did the CMR cross the conventional threshold for emergencies. Nevertheless, contrary to most previous emergencies where children have been the most vulnerable (Toole, 1996), data here suggest that the elderly may have been most at risk for both war-related trauma and overall increased mortality.

Questions and Challenges for Collecting Mortality Data in Future Humanitarian Emergencies

Recent crises in Kosovo, Bosnia and elsewhere outside of Africa have led to a call to change the mortality definition of an emergency and to recognize the altered epidemiological profile that has been demonstrated in these circumstances (Waldman and Martone, 1999). The experience of collecting mortality data for the Kosovo crisis provided useful information but raised questions of how to respond to this call. Furthermore, it raises several methodological issues that need to be addressed if we are to improve our understanding and techniques of health surveillance.

1. Should mortality still be considered the most sensitive indicator of an emergency-affected population's health status? The CMR in FYROM (and probably also in Albania) did not appear to be elevated for the refugees, but few humanitarian workers would deny that they faced a public health crisis. This issue raises the further question of whether emergency surveillance systems should focus primarily on morbidity and detecting epidemics in certain situations where mortality appears low.

2. Similarly, in low CMR situations, what is the appropriate threshold to define significant excess mortality? Obviously, the previous standard of 1 death per 10,000 per day is not sensitive enough to detect major increases in mortality among populations with comparatively low pre-emergency rates. We need to consider whether a doubling of baseline rates may be an appropriate definition in these circumstances.

3. How do we monitor mortality in non-camp settings? Most refugee deaths in Albania and FYROM occurred in hospitals, not in camps where

emergency surveillance systems were operational. In FYROM the government required that mortality be reported through the routine surveillance system, which resulted in lengthy delays in obtaining potentially critical health data. Separate registration and reporting systems for refugees admitted to hospitals should be instituted but may be problematic in many situations. Agencies in charge of surveillance in emergency settings must be willing to commit additional resources to bolster routine systems and provide expedited reporting.

4. How do we calculate denominators in situations of massive population flows, particularly when many refugees may be housed with local populations? When populations shift over short periods of time, should the midpoint or average population be used as a denominator in calculating CMR? Do we need to account for situations of rapid in- and out-migration where the total population remains the same, but the population turnover is high? Epidemiologists involved in emergencies have developed some techniques for cross-sectional population estimations, but we need to discuss with demographers how to further develop these tools and address calculating denominators.

5. Cluster sampling, which was developed to measure immunization coverage, has routinely been used for retrospective mortality surveys. Can both the sampling and analysis of this methodology be refined to reflect the non-homogenous pattern of deaths in crisis situations? Beyond the questions inherent in estimating populations and determining clusters, does this method offer the precision needed to document relatively rare events such as deaths? Epidemiologists, demographers, and survey statisticians need to collaborate on answering these and other questions to improve practical methods of mortality surveillance in emergencies.

REFERENCES

Albanian Ministry of Health Statistic Unit
    1999   Number of deaths among refugees in Albanian hospitals (4/1/99 to 6/3/99).
Alkan, M.
    1999   Personal communication. Israeli Military Field Hospital, Brazda camp.
Ascherio, A., R. Chase, T. Cote, G. Dehaes, E. Hoskins, J. Laaouej, M. Passey, S. Qaderi, S. Shuqaidef, and M.C. Smith
    1992   Effect of the Gulf War on infant and child mortality in Iraq. *New England Journal of Medicine* 327(13):931-936.
Beckman, H.
    1999   Personal communication. German Red Cross Field Hospital, Brazda camp.
Coulombier, D.
    1999   Personal communication. Institut de Veille Sanitaire, November 22, 1999.
del Mundo, F., and R. Wilkinson
    1999   A race against time. *Refugees* 3(116):4-15.

El Hillal
1999   Request for funeral expenses submitted to UNHCR, June 1, 1999.
Former Yugoslav Republic of Macedonia Ministry of the Interior
1999   Line listing of refugee deaths, March-June, 1999.
Instituti Shendetit Publik and World Health Organization
1999   Surveillance system among Kosovar refugee population in Albania: Final report.
       World Health Organization/European Regional Office.
International Organization for Migration
1999   IOM/UNHCR registration database accessed on May 27, 1999.
Kosovo Institute of Public Health
1997   Statistical Report, 1997.
Ministry of Health of the Republic of Albania, World Health Organization Humanitarian
       Mission, Tirana, and Institut de Veille Sanitaire
1999   Kosovar Refugee Information System (KRYSIS) weekly reports from April 16-
       June 6, 1999.
Perea W.
1999   Report on rapid needs assessment among Kosovar refugees hosted by Albanian
       families, and assessment of human rights violations committed in Kosovo. Paris:
       Epicentre.
Sphere Project Steering Committee for Humanitarian Response and Interaction
1998   Sphere Project Report. Geneva, 1998.
Spiegel, P.B., and P. Salama
2000   War and mortality in Kosovo, 1998-99: An epidemiological testimony. *Lancet*
       355:2204-2209.
Toole, M.J.
1996   Vulnerability in emergency situations. *Lancet* 348(9031):840.
United States Agency for International Development
1999   USAID Fact Sheet #72, June 15, 1999. [Online]. Available: http://
       www.info.usaid.gov [Accessed: June 17, 1999.]
Valenciano, M., A. Pinto, D. Coulombier, E. Hashorva, and M. Murthi
1999   Surveillance of communicable diseases among Kosovar refugees in Albania.
       Eurosurveillance, Sept 1999. [Online]. Available: http://www.cese.org/
       eurosurv_eng.htm [Accessed: November 1, 1999].
Waldman, R., and G. Martone
1999   Public health and complex emergencies: New issues, new conditions. *American
       Journal of Public Health* 89(10):1483-1485.
World Health Organization Regional Office for Europe, Office for Humanitarian Assistance
       of the FYROM, and the Health Information Network for Advanced Planning
1999   Health Bulletins from April 26-July 2, 1999 (Nos. 5-14).

5

The Demographic Analysis of Mortality Crises: The Case of Cambodia, 1970-1979

Patrick Heuveline

As best as can now be estimated, over two million Cambodians died during the 1970s because of the political events of the decade, the vast majority of them during the mere four years of the "Khmer Rouge" regime. This number of deaths is even more staggering when related to the size of the Cambodian population, then less than eight million. In my estimation, about a third of the 1970 population would have survived to the end of the decade under "normal" demographic conditions but did not under the circumstances that prevailed. No single factor alone explains the rare intensity of the Cambodian mortality crisis. Instead, the excess mortality pattern reflects one of the worst imaginable mixes of conditions, including war casualties, massive population displacement, ethnic cleansing, health system collapse, and famine.

I begin this chapter with a brief summary of the various political events that had demographic consequences in the 1970s. I continue with a discussion of the different sources of data and corresponding techniques for estimating the volume of deaths during a mortality crisis. I then discuss further the estimation of the cause-of-death, sex and age patterns of crisis mortality. To illustrate how particular conditions and data availability constrain the choice of methods and the implementation of the selected methods, the last section describes past estimations of mortality patterns in Cambodia during the 1970s.

CAMBODIA IN THE 1970s[1]

At the onset of this terrible decade in Cambodian history, the Communist Party of Kampuchea's (CPK) armed opposition to prince Norodom Sihanouk was gaining momentum. Those who would be remembered as the "Khmers Rouges," a term coined by Sihanouk himself, occupied bases in the northeast and northwest corners of the country from which they rendered unsafe as much as a fifth of Cambodia's territory (Chandler, 1996). To the west, Vietnamese communist troops held bases on Cambodian soil. Up to this point, the population of Cambodia can be reasonably well extrapolated from the demographic analysis of its 1962 census (Migozzi, 1973; Siampos, 1970).

In March 1970, the National Assembly voted Sihanouk out of power to the benefit of his own Prime Minister, Lon Nol. Sihanouk learned of the coup while on holiday, out of the country. With the support of North Vietnam, he took command of an opposition alliance whose military force on the ground consisted mostly of his former foes of the CPK. In part because of the North Vietnamese support to the opposition, the new Cambodian government started a strong campaign against the half million ethnic Vietnamese then living in Cambodia and suspected of supporting Sihanouk. The Cambodian army killed thousands of Vietnamese civilians (Chandler, 1996:205), and about 300,000 people are believed to have fled—or to have been expelled by force—to Vietnam during the first eight months of 1970 (Migozzi, 1973:44). But the inexperienced and ill-equipped army failed to drive North Vietnamese forces out of the country.

Over the next four years, the Lon Nol government gradually lost control over the Cambodian countryside. The mortality impact of the civil war is difficult to assess, but the main controversy in this respect concerns the impact of a massive bombardment of eastern Cambodia by U.S. planes in early 1973—sometimes referred to as the "Kissinger war" because of former U.S. Secretary of State Henry Kissinger's involvement— meant to weaken the North Vietnamese troops. Sihanouk (1986:144) mentions a widely circulated but unsubstantiated estimate that 700,000 Cambodians were killed under the Lon Nol government. Kiernan (1989) argues that the impact of the U.S. bombing could not be more than 150,000 deaths, and subsequent reevaluations of the demographic data situated

---

[1] Although more emphasis is given here to deaths and refugees movements, the historical account in this section borrows liberally from Chandler (1996), to which the reader is referred for more details about the political developments of the decade. For an unforgettable, personal account of the post-1975 period, see Ung (2000). For a discussion of the available demographic data, see Huguet (1992), Banister and Johnson (1993), and Heuveline (1998a).

the death toll for the four years in the order of 300,000 or less (Banister and Johnson, 1993:87-90; Sliwinski, 1995:48).

The Khmers Rouges took Phnom Penh in April 1975. The population of the capital had swollen with the influx of about two million refugees that had moved with the front. One of the first decisions of the new Democratic Kampuchea (DK) was to empty the cities, pushing the formerly urban population on the road to rural areas with no delay or explanation. While food shortages were looming, political purposes likely motivated the decision (Chandler, 1996:210). Forced to walk along long roads, these "new people"—by opposition to rural people, referred to as "base" people in the DK revolutionary terms—began to experience what would be their lot for the four years of the DK: exhaustion, lack of food, and executions. Due to long days of physical labor, exposure to deadly malaria strains, and insufficient food rations, the mortality of the relocated "new people" was dramatic, in particular for the sick, the elderly, and youngest children. The Khmers Rouges also engaged in political and ethnic purges against those connected to the Lon Nol government and former ruling elite, the remaining ethnic Vietnamese, the Muslim Chams, and more generally all those deemed enemies of the revolution (Kiernan, 1996). Mortality increase was not contained to any specific sub-population, however. As early as 1976, food was scarce for the entire civilian population as the food produced was allocated in priority to the troops and even exported to generate revenues to pay back arms. The sanitary conditions deteriorated as clinics lost their trained medical staff and medicine supplies. Executions could punish any minor violations of the Khmers Rouges' orders as well as internal dissension within the party ranks.

From the beginning, the DK maintained a defiant attitude toward Vietnam but the tensions escalated rapidly toward the end of 1977. After a first successful penetration into Cambodia in December 1977, followed by a voluntary withdrawal a few weeks later, Vietnamese troops entered Cambodia again at the end of 1978. This time they continued toward Phnom Penh, reaching as early as January 1979 a capital abandoned by the Khmers Rouges for the north and northwest mountains. As the Khmers Rouges retreated, many Cambodians returned to their original residence or moved to search for family members from whom they had been separated. An unfortunate consequence was that much of the crops were left untended, which combined with a drought and the lack of food stocks from previous years to create dramatic food shortages that impacted all the more a population already exhausted by years of bare subsistence. An international campaign was quickly launched to send relief to Cambodia but was hampered by a destroyed infrastructure and various bureaucratic constraints. Food supply remained deficient for most of 1979 and the famine could not be completely avoided. The most dramatic estimates of its toll are around 500,000 deaths (Ea, 1987; Banister and Johnson, 1993; Sliwinski, 1995) but those are again contested as much too high (Kiernan, 1986).

As the DK was closed to foreigners and did not maintain national statistics, for a while no quantitative estimate of mortality during the DK was available. Some demographic data on the population of Cambodia became available in the early 1980s. Suspicions about the quality of these data arose because they were mere administrative counts that served political purposes, by entering into the regional allocation scheme of international aid (Huguet, 1992). Moreover, tallying population estimates from local registers must have been quite difficult at a time of high population mobility. Better data became available in the 1990s, starting with the 1993 electoral lists (United Nations, 1995), the 1996 Demographic Survey, and the 1998 General Population Census (National Institute of Statistics, 1996; National Institute of Statistics, 1999).

Estimates were derived from these data by the methods discussed in the next section but they vary tremendously, with respect to overall mortality as well as to the particular contribution of the executions (Heuveline, 1998b). The pro-Vietnamese government of the 1980s claimed that the Khmers Rouges were accountable for three million lives. At the low end of the range, an estimate of one million victims has widely circulated in the Western press. While the figure is consistent with some demographic accounts (Ea, 1981; Vickery, 1988; Banister and Johnson, 1993), most estimates now cluster around one and a half to two million deaths (Sliwinski, 1995; Kiernan, 1996; Heder, 1997; Heuveline, 1998a). There is even more disagreement concerning the number of executions. While Ea (1981) considers they numbered at most 120,000, most analysts believe they accounted for a third to one half of excess mortality during the period, thus 500,000 to 1 million deaths (Vickery, 1988; Sliwinski, 1995; Kiernan, 1996; Heder, 1997; Heuveline, 1998a).

Many people also fled the country, most often westward to Thailand, and sometimes by sea. The number of those who survived the dangers of the sea or the landmines is relatively well recorded in refugee camps statistics. The number of refugees repatriated from Thailand by the United Nations High Commissioner for Refugees (UNHCR) on the eve of the 1993 elections[2] was nearly 400,000 (United Nations, 1995), whereas about 200,000 more refugees emigrated abroad, foremost to Australia, France, and the United States. The number of those who fled toward Vietnam and stayed there is more difficult to estimate, but except for

---

[2] This number is higher than the number of people who had emigrated from Cambodia because of the fast population growth of the population in refugee camps (on the order of 4 percent annually).

what was left of the ethnic Vietnamese population in 1975 (about 200,000 people), this was not the most likely destination as civilians were pushed westward by the moving military front. (For a fuller description of migration data, see Banister and Johnson, 1993.) Finally, fertility appears to have begun falling in the early 1970s, and from 1975 on, the decline has been fairly drastic. The size of adjacent age groups in the 1998 census data suggests that the annual number of births could have been reduced to between one-half to three-fourths of antebellum levels, implying a deficit in these four years in the order of 300,000 to 600,000 births.

DATA SOURCES AND MORTALITY ESTIMATION

Vital Statistics

Continuous registration of deaths is the preferred source of data when the recording is believed to be accurate and complete. Several methods can be used, depending on the nature of ancillary data, to assess the completeness of mortality registers (e.g., Chandra Sekar and Deming, 1949; Brass, 1975; Preston and Hill, 1980; for a description of these and other techniques see Preston et al., 2001).

There are reasons to doubt the availability and quality of vital statistics during mortality crises. Registration systems are typically maintained by civil servants. The crisis can be expected to disrupt the recording of vital events, either because political upheavals means a change of personnel with a period of vacancy, or because the crisis is so intense that record keeping takes a low priority. The Khmers Rouges proved to be capable of accurate record keeping as shown by the chilling records of jail administrators (Kiernan, 1996). They apparently did not attempt to achieve complete national vital statistics, however, and the demographic data they released reflected more their propaganda strategy than their statistical efforts. More reliable death statistics might be available from an external administration, such as those on refugee populations in UNHCR-administered camps. Other chapters in this volume may offer such examples. But most often, continuous recording during mortality crises should be expected to provide data that are too partial—in both meanings of the term—to be reliable.

Census Data

A general census may include questions to the household heads about the selected characteristics of any past household member deceased in the 12 months before the census. These data can occasionally provide a complete count of deaths in countries without complete vital registration but accurate periodical censuses. In practice, this approach has not proved most reliable. Precisely in places where death registration is not common, respondents may not remember well the date of death and deaths can be wrongly included in or omitted from the recall period. Since the likelihood of false inclusion and omission typically vary with the age of the deceased, the age pattern of deaths thus reported is not reliable either.

This approach is even more problematic to use for the retrospective evaluation of a mortality crisis. The first reason is that it may take years after the crisis for a government to have the capacity to conduct a complete household census operation, and the longer the time elapsed since the events, the less reliable the retrospective data are. When the crisis is associated with military conflict, a census conducted shortly after the events might have to exclude some zones that are still unsafe, as was the case in Cambodia in the early 1980s (and in fact through the late 1990s). This may introduce a selection bias since such zones might have been disproportionately affected by the conflict during the period of interest. Finally, the approach implicitly assumes some stability in household membership, which may not hold when many people are displaced. The retrospective questions may instead concern a fixed set of family members, for instance, biological parents, siblings, and children, instead of household members but then this raises concerns about possible double counting, especially when mortality is very high.

Sample Survey Data

Similar retrospective questions can be asked to a sample of respondents. The sample-based approach is of course much easier to implement than the census-based one and under certain conditions the results can be confidently extrapolated to the entire population. These conditions are difficult to meet in post-crisis situations that typically prevent the use of traditional sampling procedures. This might be particularly problematic when the mortality risks and patterns vary substantially across sub-populations, as was the case in Cambodia among ethnic minorities and, among Khmers, between the new and base people, or simply across regions differently affected by the civil war. To begin with, the distribution of the Cambodian population by relevant characteristics such as those above was not that well documented at the onset of the civil war. Thus, the relative size of the different "risk groups" can be only roughly estimated. Moreover, if the interviews take place shortly after the events, some subgroups are likely to be less accessible than others are, and the selected sample is likely to be a sample of convenience rather than a random sample with desirable statistical properties. Often, the survey takers will be restricted to a few areas of easier access or worse, if the country is still inaccessible, to the refugee population. If the original population is universally at risk, the refugees may constitute a selected sub-population, since those who stay behind continue to be exposed to that risk. In other situations, on the contrary, the refugees might have been those most at risk and thus most likely to flee.

Another type of selection effect is that at least one of the immediate relatives of a person must be alive at the time of the survey for that person's experience (death or survival) to be recorded. In other words, the probability of inclusion in the sample is conditional on the survival of parents, children, and siblings. This introduces a bias as long as the survival probabilities of close family members are related, which was clearly the case in Cambodia as probably in most such mortality crises whichever their causes. In the event of the execution of an entire family (both parents and all their children), for instance, the death of the children could not be recorded by this method, while the death of the parents could only be recorded if one of their own parents or siblings survived. In general, those with surviving immediate relatives are more likely to have survived themselves. This "clustering" of mortality within families might be negligible under most normal conditions but becomes problematic when a sizeable share of deaths are due to politically or ethnically motivated executions or bombardment of villages.

With typically small sample sizes, double counting is probably not as important an issue as in a census-based operation. But the sample-based approach is susceptible of the same recall errors as mentioned above for the census questions. Concerning such dramatic events, it is less likely that respondents would not remember what happened or when it did since the reference recall period can be delineated by salient events. In many emergency situations, though, it is possible that respondents would not know what happened even to close family members. In Cambodia, it took years for members of dispersed families to reunite. According to Sliwinski's 1989-1991 data, 12.5 percent of the relatives reported as presumed or known to have died in 1975-1979 were in fact still missing at that time (Sliwinski, 1995:60).

The sample approach, with retrospective questions on immediate family members, has a number of methodological shortcomings. It cannot be overemphasized, however, that this is often the only technique that can be implemented by a lone investigator and a few collaborators very shortly after the mortality crisis. It thus provides invaluable preliminary estimates when other techniques are much harder and costlier to implement.

Two Population Estimates

When there are no registration or retrospective data on deaths, mortality can be estimated indirectly from relationships between different demographic variables. Most of these so-called indirect estimation techniques cannot be used in the analysis of mortality crisis because the estimation of one variable from another one relies on some empirical regularity in the relationship between the two variables across populations. These empirical regularities are embedded in demographic models that often cannot be applied to the populations of interest here, precisely because of the exceptional nature of the situations these populations have been exposed to.

One demographic relationship that applies to all populations no matter how exceptional the circumstances is often referred to as the balancing equation of population change. This accounting identity basically expresses that there are only two ways to leave a population, emigration and death, and two ways to enter it, immigration and birth. Thus the change in population size between two dates, $P(t)$ and $P(t+n)$, depends on four flows: births, $B(t,t+n)$; deaths, $D(t,t+n)$; immigration, $I(t,t+n)$; and emigration, $O(t,t+n)$, or

$$P(t+n) = P(t) + B(t,t+n) - D(t,t+n) + I(t,t+n) - O(t,t+n) \qquad (1)$$

If population estimates by age and sex were available just at the beginning and the end of the period of interest, this logic could be used to study the mortality of people already born at the beginning of the period. The most common strategy is to follow birth cohorts over their life course (along diagonals in a Lexis diagram, see Figure 5-1). Equation (2) expresses that changes in the size of a birth cohort result only from migrations and deaths of cohort members:

$$_nP_x(t+n) = {}_nP_{x-n}(t) - {}_nD^c_{t-x}(t,t+n) + {}_nI^c_{t-x}(t,t+n) - {}_nO^c_{t-x}(t,t+n) \qquad (2)$$

where $_nP_{x-n}(t)$ and $_nP_x(t+n)$ are, respectively, the number of people aged $x-n$ to x at time t and aged x to $x+n$ at time $t+n$, and $_nD^c_{t-x}(t,t+n)$, $_nI^c_{t-x}(t,t+n)$, and $_nO^c_{t-x}(t,t+n)$ are, respectively, the number of deaths, in-migrations, and out-migrations between time t and $t+n$ of people born between time $t-x-n$ and $t-x$. Equation (2) simply restricts the terms in Equation (1) to certain birth cohorts, and for those cohorts that are already born at time t, there is no fertility term in Equation (2).

If there is no migration, the remaining two terms in the right-hand side of Equation (2) correspond to the number of survivors at time $t+n$ among the birth cohort survivors at time t. This is often expressed as a

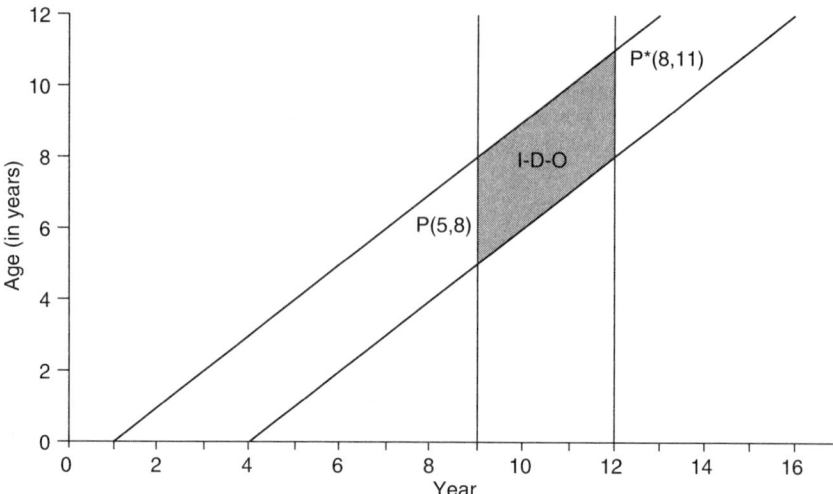

FIGURE 5-1   Illustration of the cohort-component estimation of population change. Note: P(5,8) is the population aged 5 to 8 in year 9 and P*(8,11) is the population aged 8 to 11 in year 12. I, D, and O are, respectively, the numbers of in-migrations, deaths, and out-migrations between year 9 and 12, of people born between year 1 and year 4 (with reference to time and birth cohort dropped for notational simplicity.)

life-table survival ratio, as suggested by Coale and Demeny (United Nations, 1983):

$$_nP_x(t+n) = {}_nP_{x-n}(t) - {}_nD^c_{t-x}(t,t+n) = {}_nP_{x-n}(t) * [{}_nL_x/{}_nL_{x-n} (t,t+n)]   \qquad (3)$$

Equation (3) provides the basis of a simple method for constructing a life table for the period.[3]   This approach requires that the length of the period be equal to the width of the age group or multiples thereof. This requirement can be waived with so-called variable-r techniques that compare the size of the same age group at two different times ($_nP_x(t+n)$ and $_nP_x(t)$ with the above notations). These techniques will not be described in details here but when the length of period is a multiple of the width of the

---

[3] Coale and Demeny (United Nations, 1983) also suggest to work with successive open age groups (e.g., age five and above, age ten and above, etc.) rather than with closed age groups in order to minimize the effects of age misstatement at older ages.

age group, these techniques are exactly equivalent to those based on changes in cohort size.[4]

Whether the cohort or age-group approach is chosen, these techniques only estimate the mortality of those born at the beginning of the period, and the corresponding life table starts at age n, where n is the length of the crisis period. To obtain mortality estimates from birth requires data on birth during the period. Such data are often unavailable and it is also problematic to assess how much the mortality crisis might have affected reproductive behavior. In Cambodia, for instance, fertility in the worst years might have declined down to half its pre-crisis level.[5]

The population totals at the onset and at the end of the events of interest, $P(t)$ and $P(t+n)$, are seldom directly available and need to be estimated from population data pertaining to earlier and later dates. When statistics are available and reliable up to the onset of the period, the extrapolation of the population $P(t)$ can proceed in an additive manner from the last population size estimate and the different flows in and out of the population between the time of that last estimate and time t as in Equation (1). When these flows cannot be estimated directly, population $P(t)$ can be best estimated by a forward projection, with the cohort-component technique detailed in standard demography textbooks (e.g., Shryock and Siegel, 1975; Preston et al., 2001). The forward projection does not require exact counts of births and deaths but instead indicators of fertility and mortality levels (e.g., total fertility rate and life expectancy at birth), together with models of fertility and mortality by age, and the initial age structure of the population. In the pre-crisis period, several indirect techniques can provide the required estimates of fertility and mortality levels from incomplete vital statistics (United Nations, 1983).

Similarly, the population at the end of the crisis period must be estimated. This can be done by calculating a backward population projection from any post-crisis population estimate. Although backward projections may be less intuitive than forward ones, the process is quite similar. The data requirements are slightly less intensive, because the number of births in a given period is implied by the number of people under a certain age alive at the end of the period and by their mortality and migration rates. Fertility rates are not needed.

If migration can be accurately estimated, these techniques can still be

---

[4] For a description of some variable-r techniques, the reader is referred to United Nations (1983) and Preston et al. (2001).

[5] A gradual fertility reduction, reaching at its trough about 50 percent of pre-crisis fertility levels, was also observed in China (Ashton et al., 1984). For a review of demographic responses to short-term shocks, see Lee (1997:1078-85).

used by adjusting $_nP_{x-n}(t)$ and $_nP_x(t+n)$ before entering them in Equation (3).[6] When the mortality crisis is associated with a massive displacement of people, uncertainty about population movements can make this method useless. Note, however, that only the difference between immigration and emigration during the period, in other terms the *net* total of migrants during the period, affects the left-hand side estimate in Equation (2).

The logic of indirect estimation using the balancing equation of population change is similar to assembling a jigsaw puzzle with a single missing piece, whose size and shape can be revealed by fitting together the remaining pieces. But most often, the other pieces can only be estimated more or less precisely, and the size and shape of the missing piece only appears fuzzy. The quality of the estimation thus depends on the precision of the other pieces of demographic information. Direct estimation with survey data is sensitive to the estimated mid-period population size that is required to translate the estimated proportion of deaths among the sample's relatives into a total number of deaths in the population. Indirect techniques with two population estimates are sensitive to the underestimation or overestimation of population size at the beginning of the period *relative* to population size at the end of the period, and to migration, the other cause of changes in cohort size.[7]

NATURAL AND CRISIS MORTALITY PATTERNS

In this section, I discuss likely changes in mortality patterns during mortality crises. A mortality crisis is not defined exactly but it refers to a situation where mortality increases suddenly. Pre-crisis mortality trends will be referred to as "normal" mortality and the difference between the prevailing crisis mortality and the mortality extrapolated to the crisis period from normal mortality trends will be referred to as "excess" mortality. When the level of mortality increases sharply, mortality patterns can often be expected to change as well, that is, the distribution of death (by sex, by age, by cause, by region, by ethnic group, etc.) is also likely to be modified. Demographers and actuaries have long documented the

---

[6] A common population projection strategy consists of adding half of the net number of migrants aged x to x+n in the period t to t+n to the population aged x to x+n at time t and the other half to the population aged x to x+n at time t+n. This arithmetic approximation is not entirely consistent with the projection framework based on rates but the numerical implications of this slight inconsistency are usually not important.

[7] Note that an underestimation of, say, mortality both before and after the crisis period would lead to underestimate population size at the beginning of the period (in the forward projection from census date 1) and to overestimate population size at the end of the period (in the backward projection from census date 2).

typical sex, age, and cause-of-death patterns of normal mortality and I concentrate here on changes in these patterns during mortality crises. (For a discussion of the ethnic and regional mortality patterns during the Cambodian crisis, see Kiernan, 1996.)

Age Patterns

The time-honored tradition of studying mortality at different ages established that in most human populations mortality follows a "J-pattern," namely that it decreases from birth to a minimum before sexual maturity and then increases with age. Demographers have thus attempted to capture this empirical regularity in mathematical functions (mortality law) or tabular representations with few parameters that account for interpopulation variations associated with their specific environments (e.g., diet or exposure to infectious agents). In one of the most commonly used examples, Coale and Demeny (1983) system of model life tables, these variations are represented by four different "regional" patterns. Each model pattern consists of a set of life tables, with each table providing mortality rates corresponding to a given level of mortality (i.e., a summary indicator of mortality such as life expectancy at birth).

These life tables have become central to the direct and indirect techniques of mortality estimation. Because age reporting is deficient in many populations, demographers usually prefer to assume that the age pattern is one of the existing model built from reliable sources and to concentrate on the estimation of the level of mortality. For instance, registered or reported data on deaths by age can be "smoothed" with a model age pattern of mortality (United Nations, 1983). When using the techniques based on two population estimates, it is also suggested to select a model pattern and record the level implied by each cohort or age group. To select the model life table whose level best matches those recorded across cohorts or age groups is often thought more reliable than to put together the mortality rates obtained from each cohort or each age group.

These empirical similarities in mortality age patterns reflect human populations' common experience of so-called "natural" causes of death and are expected as long as such natural mortality dominates. Mortality also comprises "accidental" mortality—labeled as such by opposition to natural mortality—that typically includes suicide, homicide, and unintentional injuries. These causes of death—thereafter referred to as "violent" mortality—do not necessarily follow the overall J-pattern of mortality but they typically account for a small fraction of all-age deaths and do not affect the overall age pattern. In mortality crises such that the vulnerability of the population to natural mortality increases dramatically with little change in the proportion of deaths due to violent mortality, model

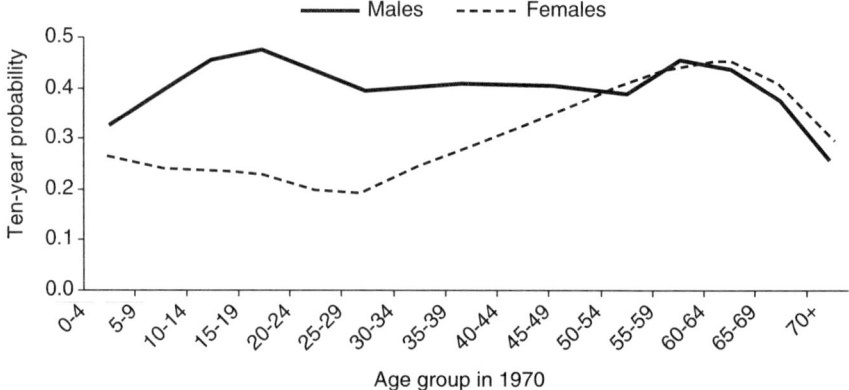

FIGURE 5-2   Sex and age pattern of mortality in Cambodia, ten-year probability of dying, 1970-1979. Source: Heuveline (1998a).

age patterns of mortality and the methods built thereon should still be applicable. Model life tables based on data from medium-to-low mortality populations do not seem to provide a very good extrapolation of mortality patterns under higher mortality conditions (Bhat, 1987), however, and the analyst should preferably turn to model age patterns specifically designed for high-mortality populations (Preston et al., 1993).

On the contrary, when violent mortality becomes an important part of overall mortality, the mortality pattern may have little in common with the nearly universal J-pattern and model age patterns cannot be used. Figure 5-2, for instance, presents the age pattern of excess mortality estimated for Cambodian males and females during the 1970s. These age patterns of mortality, especially the male one, bear no resemblance with any model age pattern. This finding is not particularly surprising since wartime life tables are typically excluded from the empirical basis on which the model age patterns are constructed (e.g., Coale and Demeny, 1983). The reason is precisely that the age pattern of war-related deaths differs from that of natural mortality and reflects idiosyncratic conditions at a particular time and place that should not be generalized to other populations.

Decomposition by Cause

Existing model age patterns of mortality can not be used to assess and improve the quality of such an unusual age pattern of mortality as shown in Figure 5-2. But the unusual aspect of this age pattern is also useful because the departure from the original pattern is caused by the rise of a few formerly rare causes of death, typically associated with the mortality crisis. Mortality age patterns thus reflect the prevalence of different causes of death in the population (Preston, 1976) and below I discuss an approximate breakdown between mortality from natural causes from violent causes. A simpler decomposition between normal and excess mortality is presented first.

The idea of both decompositions is to return to Equation (2) but to further decompose the number of deaths, $D(t,t+n)$, as the sum of a first component that one can estimate, $D^*(t,t+n)$, and a residual component that one tries to estimate, $E(t,t+n)$. In the case of a mortality crisis, for instance, we could estimate the number of excess deaths from change in population size and other flows during the period, including the number of deaths due to normal mortality, as shown in Equation (4):

$$E(t,t+n)=P(t) - P(t+n) + B(t,t+n) - D^*(t,t+n) + I(t,t+n) - O(t,t+n) \qquad (4)$$

where $E(t,t+n)$ is now the number of excess deaths and $D^*(t,t+n)$ the expected number of deaths under normal mortality conditions in the period t to $t+n$.

Just as Equation (3) restricts Equation (2) to certain birth cohorts, Equation (4) can be applied separately to different birth cohorts, an approach developed originally to estimate international migration (Shryock and Siegel, 1975:595-6):

$$_n\Delta_x(t+n) = {}_nP_x(t+n) - {}_nP_{x-n}(t) * [{}_nL_x/{}_nL_{x-n} (t,t+n)] \qquad (5a)$$

where $_n\Delta_x(t+n)$ is the residual difference at time $t+n$ among people aged x to $x+n$, that is, a residual term in the forward projection of $_nP_{x-n}(t)$ to time $t+n$. The residual term is not exactly the number of people who died from excess mortality or migrated during the period. It is more exactly the number of people missing (in case of excess mortality or predominantly out-migration) at the end of the period. In a growing population, the residual term at the end of the period overestimates the additional deaths or migrations because the number of people added to (or subtracted from) the population during the period contributed to (or would have contributed to) the growth of the population till the end of the period. A numerically satisfactory solution suggested by Shryock and Siegel is to also compute:

$$_n\Delta_x(t) = {}_nP_x(t) - {}_nP_{x+n}(t+n) * [{}_nL_x/{}_nL_{x+n} (t,t+n)] \qquad (5b)$$

and to take the average of $_n\Delta_x(t)$ and $_n\Delta_x(t+n)$ as the net number of excess deaths or migrations of people aged x to $x+n$ in the period.

As in the case of total mortality estimation, the assessment of excess mortality can be implemented by age groups rather than by cohorts. This approach was introduced, again in the context of international migration, by Hill (1987), who also discusses the advantages and disadvantages of the two approaches. For either approach to be applied to a decomposition of mortality, the beginning and the end populations must be adjusted for international migrations using ancillary data.[8] Then, survival ratios must be selected to represent either normal or natural mortality. The selection of normal mortality survival ratios can be based on a simple extrapolation of pre-crisis mortality trends. The residual number of deaths is readily interpreted as excess mortality.

A second decomposition, based on the same logic, is perhaps less compelling, but it considers two main types of death during the mortality crisis. The first type corresponds to the stark increase in natural mortality and includes all biological causes of death that became more prevalent because of a combination of harder environment (e.g., in Cambodia, malaria, sanitation in general), a weakened population (e.g., physical labor, food deficiency), and a near absence of medical remedies. The second one corresponds to violent mortality, which in Cambodia included war casualties such as combat deaths, bombardment or mines victims, and executions. To the extent that the pattern of the first type of mortality bears some similarity with age patterns of normal mortality embodied in the existing model age patterns while the pattern of the second type of mortality does not, a decomposition might be attempted based on the age structure of overall mortality.

The idea of this decomposition is thus to simulate the increase of natural mortality by selecting the model age pattern of mortality with the highest mortality level (e.g., lowest survival ratios) consistent with the pre- and post-crisis population data. This natural mortality pattern replaces normal mortality in Equations (5a) and (5b), and the new residual difference now corresponds to violent deaths only, instead of all excess deaths. The highest possible level is obtained when all deaths are accounted for in a given cohort (a higher mortality level would then predict too few people at the second date among that cohort). In other age groups, residual numbers of deaths remains positive and refer to deaths that could not be explained by an increase in natural causes of death. On the one hand, some natural deaths are likely to remain in the residual component because the actual pattern of natural mortality may have deviated from the model pattern. On the other hand, it is unlikely that any age group

---

[8] Just like the mortality estimation techniques, the decompositions are sensitive to the relative underestimation of population size at one time relative to its size at the other time. Hill (1987) suggests a technique to separate the relative underestimation from international migration. This technique can be applied to excess mortality but would work better the more the age pattern of excess mortality differs from the expected age pattern of relative underestimation.

experienced no violent mortality at all and the decomposition pushes natural mortality to its lowest possible level. Even though these two possible biases would partially compensate one another, the decomposition is only indicative of the relative share of the two mortality types.

It is not entirely clear *a priori* whether deaths from famine should be considered part of natural mortality in this decomposition. On one hand, they could be considered separately because it is a category of death virtually absent under normal conditions that in Cambodia, for instance, rose to 35.4 percent of all reported deaths according to survey data (Sliwinski, 1995). On the other hand, famine may be considered as the extreme form of malnutrition, which intertwines with natural causes-of-death (e.g., Martorell and Ho, 1984). Since the decomposition is based on the difference in age patterns, the answer depends mostly on whether the age pattern of famine mortality is similar to that of natural mortality.

Famine mortality has been observed to most affect the youngest (after weaning) and the oldest persons, during European famines (e.g., Lebrun, 1971) as well as during more recent ones in Asia (Ashton et al., 1984; Maharatna, 1996). The observation is sustained by data collected by Sliwinski (1995) from Cambodian survivors about their relatives that died, with death reported in one of five categories: natural causes, famine, execution, war-related injuries, and missing (or unknown cause). As expected, the pattern of natural mortality follows the usual J-pattern even in these exceptional circumstances (Figure 5-3). The last three categories correspond to violent mortality (people still "missing" at the time of the survey ten years later had likely been executed without the knowledge of their immediate relatives, an assumption supported by the similar age patterns of the two categories). Among those, executions constitute the most frequent category, with 37.5 percent of all reported deaths, and they exhibit an age pattern quite distinct from that of natural mortality by peaking during adulthood (war-related injuries, a lesser category not shown on Figure 5-3, do so at even younger adult ages). Mortality due to natural causes and mortality due to famine mortality also have similar patterns, except that famine mortality continues to decrease into adulthood. This translation of the mortality minimum between natural causes and famine might be due to a particular feature of the social organization of the DK, namely that food rations were allocated based on the perceived value of the individual to the society. Soldiers were a priority and productive adults in general received more appropriate food than children did.

ESTIMATIONS OF EXCESS MORTALITY IN CAMBODIA

Vital registration statistics in Cambodia were already incomplete before the 1970s but they were interrupted during the DK. As for direct

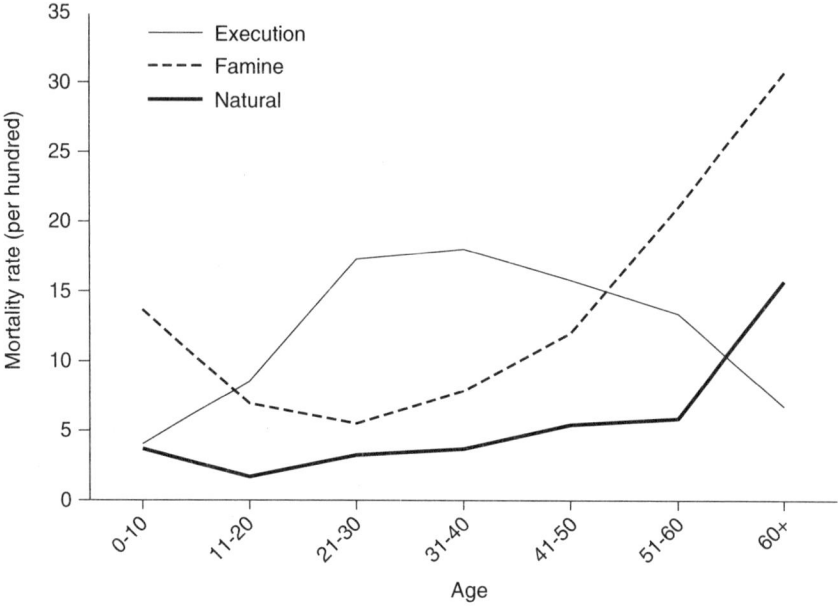

FIGURE 5-3   Age pattern of mortality from natural causes, famine, and execution in Cambodia, mortality rate, 1975-1979.   Source: Adapted from Sliwinski (1995: 52, 82).

census data on excess mortality, questions were included in an early 1980s administrative census. They resulted in an estimate of 3.3 million deaths, a tally inflated by multiple counts, the number of which could never be fully accounted for, as the records were not computerized and name matching almost impossible. Moreover, parts of the country not under governmental control could not be included, and those typically included sparsely populated but high mortality zones.

Estimation from Survey Data

Direct estimation has been mostly based on small sample survey data. As early as 1979, Ben Kiernan interviewed about 100 Cambodian immigrants in France and followed with about 400 interviews in Cambodia in 1980. Similarly, Stephen Heder conducted interviews in parts of Cambodia and at the Thai border in 1980 and 1981, obtaining separate estimates of relative loss for Khmer and ethnic Chinese "new" people (33 percent and 50 percent, respectively), and for Khmer "base" people (25 percent). Operating shortly after the fall of the DK, when many parts of the country were still unsafe, the authors must have limited themselves geographically. In spite of their efforts to stratify their estimates by reaching different segments of the population, the representativeness of their sample is difficult to assess. Even a decade later (1989-1991) when Marek Sliwinski undertook a more thorough and methodologically sophisticated study of the dead relatives of Cambodian survivors in France, in Thai border camps, and in Cambodia, safety and logistical considerations constrained his Cambodian sample to a 100-mile radius from the capital city.

In spite of the methodological shortcomings of the approach described in a section above, it is quite remarkable that both Kiernan and Heder first came up with an estimate of around one and a half million excess deaths with rudimentary techniques and what may appear to the statistically inclined reader as "cavalier" adjustments. Yet, more extensive data collected a decade or more later and with greater methodological care (1989-1991 interviews analyzed by Sliwinski; 1992-1993 electoral data analyzed by Heuveline) provided slightly higher but roughly comparable estimates. The reason is probably that a deep understanding of the local situation guided the intuition of the first authors and allowed them judicial adjustments regardless of how little justified they may appear to be on paper.

Estimation from Two Population Estimates

Several analysts have used this method to estimate excess mortality during the peak mortality period, the four years of the DK, 1975-1979 (Ea, 1981; Vickery, 1988; Banister and Johnson, 1993). All used the 1962 census to reach a population estimate for 1975 and some population data in the early 1980s (different across authors) to derive the 1979 estimate. While the authors seem to agree about a figure of excess deaths around one million, they faced several difficulties. The first one is the unreliability of the 1975 estimate thus obtained. While the population can be reasonably extrapolated from the 1962 census to 1970, the events of the early 1970s render perilous the estimation of the 1975 population that would be required to study excess mortality during the DK.

The second one relates to concerns about the reliability of the early 1980s data used by these authors. This is best illustrated by the different mid-1980 population size estimates that, in the early 1990s, still ranged from 5.7 million (U.S. Bureau of the Census, 1991:A-5) to 7.0 million (Banister and Johnson, 1993:91-3). The controversial extent of the 1979 famine poses an additional problem to the retroprojection of the population at the fall of the DK in January 1979 from population estimates in the early 1980s.

The third difficulty concerns the estimation of births in the 1975-1979 period. Even with the most recent census data (unavailable to the above authors at the time), the extent of the fertility decline can only be assessed with a fairly high level of uncertainty because the mortality conditions the 1975-1979 birth cohorts faced until the 1998 census date are not precisely known either. This uncertainty about the exact number of births (in the order of 300,000) is not at all negligible in the reconstruction since the number of deaths estimated by these authors is about one million.

As was the case with the direct methods, we must bear in mind that in spite of these limitations, the first attempts to use indirect techniques of analysis provided invaluable information on the Cambodian mortality crisis. Contrary to the situation with direct methods, though, the early estimates thus obtained disagree substantially with more recent estimates. While the early direct estimates clustered around one and a half million excess deaths, the early indirect estimates centered around one million victims. Later data led Sliwinski (1995) to a direct estimate of 1.9 million, and a reconstruction using the 1993 data yielded a central estimate of more than two million excess deaths (Heuveline, 1998a). While in any of those numerical attempts, the uncertainty is such that other estimates cannot be entirely ruled out, the estimates of one and a half million and above now appear more likely (Heuveline, 1998b).

In contrast with these previous studies also based on two population estimates, I based my analysis of Cambodian excess mortality on a 1970 population estimate and a 1980 population estimate, and I used this approach to assess excess deaths for the entire decade of the 1970s. I believe it is as accurate and more transparent to work from that estimate and subtract ancillary estimates of the death toll of the civil war and of the famine in order to obtain a tally for the DK years only. In addition, I reconstructed post-1980 trends from the electoral data gathered by the United Nations in the process of organizing the 1993 general elections (United Nations, 1995). Data of this nature are not among the typical sources of demographic analysis but those appeared to be the first national data after 1980 to be of reasonable quality and available by single year of age. In general, using data for a later date imposes to carry the backward projection on a longer time interval, which increases the uncertainty of the projected outcome. But in this particular case, it was balanced by the fact that it was easier to estimate net international migration between 1979 and 1993 than it was up to the mid-1980s, when refugee movements were still taking place.

Since the interval was ten years and the age groups five years wide, the cohort and age groups approaches were equivalent. The decomposition of normal and excess mortality is easier to conduct using the cohort approach than the age-group one because the former has been incorporated in population projection software. Since many estimates were not estimated with precision, this flexibility proved useful as it allowed for many different projections with different demographic parameters, whose outcomes mapped the range of possible estimates of excess deaths. The possibility to obtain not only a central or best estimate in the analyst's judgment, but also a sense of the uncertainty involved in the reconstruction, is a comparative advantage of the indirect approach. My specific assumptions are described below.

As in earlier studies, I began with an assessment of the 1962 census data to obtain an adjusted population sex and age structure and indirect estimates of fertility and mortality at the time (Migozzi, 1973; Siampos, 1970; Heuveline, 1998a). From 1962 to 1970, demographic trends can be assumed to be smooth: a slight decline of mortality over the period, constant fertility, and no international migration. The population by sex and five-year age groups can then be projected forward five years at a time. This yields the 1967 and 1972 populations by sex and five-year age groups, from which the January 1, 1970, population by sex and five-year age groups can be interpolated. The results, shown in Table 5-1, suggest that the population size had grown fast, from 5.7 million in 1962 to 7.7 million in 1970. For the backward projection, the population by sex and five-year age group in 1993 can also be projected backward five years at a time. An interpolation between the 1978 and 1983 estimates yields the January 1, 1980, estimates.[9] Mortality data after 1980 were poor and I simply assumed that mortality returned to its normal level quickly after the 1979 famine and resumed its pre-crisis declining trend thereafter, apparently a common feature in post-crisis situations (Murray and Chen, 1994:18).[10]

Important migrations to and from Vietnam were also poorly documented. The impact of these undocumented immigrants on the population reconstruction is limited because the 1993 electoral law barred most of the new migrants from Vietnam from registering; therefore, those who were able to register were mostly returning migrants. The timing of those movements back and forth during the period 1980-1993 may affect the population size at a given date within the period, but as mentioned earlier, the 1980 population size estimated backward from 1993 data depends only on the net number of migrants between 1980 and 1993. The same applies to the impact of the refugees to and back from Thailand,

---

[9] Only the population above age 18 was registered in the electoral data. The 1993 population is thus limited to age 20 and above. The 1978 and 1983 population estimates are limited to age five and above and ten and above, respectively. The interpolated 1980 population is thus also limited to age ten and above. This is sufficient to assess the survival of the 1970 population.

[10] In particular, this seems to have been the case in Vietnam (Banister, 1993; Barbieri et al., 1995). The situation of Vietnam is of further interest because of the similar public infrastructure in the two countries since 1980.

TABLE 5-1 Population, 1970 and 1980 and Residual Population Deficit in the 1970-80 Interval, by Age and Sex (in Thousands)

Age in 1970	1970 Population		1980 Population		Forward Projection Residual		Backward Projection Residual		Excess deaths	
	Males	Females	Males	Females	Males	Females	Males	Females	Males	Females
0-4	715.7	691.2	455.9	450.6	225.4	178.4	233.8	182.6	229.6	180.5
5-9	582.0	564.0	564.5	548.5	221.3	134.5	227.2	134.9	224.3	134.7
10-4	490.2	479.2	435.0	461.6	216.4	110.3	224.5	110.9	220.4	110.6
15-9	411.8	404.6	325.4	396.0	187.3	91.6	196.3	92.6	191.8	92.1
20-4	313.5	311.8	241.4	338.6	131.1	60.0	138.1	60.6	134.6	60.3
25-9	244.9	249.8	194.1	284.8	93.3	47.4	98.6	48.0	95.9	47.7
30-4	214.0	223.5	157.4	228.1	81.8	53.3	87.4	55.1	84.6	54.2
35-9	191.6	199.3	130.6	182.0	73.6	54.7	80.1	57.8	76.8	56.3
40-4	166.6	169.2	111.9	150.6	63.1	51.9	70.6	56.1	66.9	54.0
45-9	135.9	138.6	96.8	125.2	49.9	47.3	58.3	53.0	54.1	50.1
50-4	111.5	114.5	81.0	98.2	38.1	42.3	47.7	49.9	42.9	46.1
55-9	91.0	94.3	62.7	72.0	34.2	36.0	47.5	46.0	40.8	41.0
60-4	69.1	72.3	48.3	51.7	22.8	26.2	37.0	38.2	29.9	32.2
65-9	48.6	51.7	29.6	35.5	11.8	14.5	24.2	26.4	18.0	20.5
70+	52.5	59.5	36.3	42.7	5.0	7.3	21.6	28.0	13.3	17.7
Total	3838.8	3823.6	2971.1	3466.1	1454.9	955.7	1592.9	1040.1	1523.9	997.9

Source: Author's estimates. See Heuveline (1998a) for further details about projection parameters.

even though those would be easier to estimate yearly. Finally, the emigration of people who did not return to Cambodia by 1993 is mostly captured in the immigration statistics of receiving countries (about 250,000 after 1980). Data on the sex and age distribution of these migrants were too sketchy to use. Model age patterns of migration (Rogers and Castro, 1981) represent migration movements driven by single adults in the labor force and are not applicable when most moves are by entire families. Consistent with limited data from the refugee camp (Lynch cited in Banister and Johnson, 1993:112), the age- and sex-structure of the migrants was assumed to be that of the total population.

Even though demographic data was partly deficient to assess the post-1980 trends at the time of my analysis, more appropriate data from the 1996 Demographic Survey supported the outcomes of the backward projection. Huguet (1997) reconstructed post-1980 population dynamics with the advantage of these better data and estimated a mid-1980 population size that was 1.7 percent higher than my population size estimated for January 1, 1980 (Table 5-1).

That a population that had grown from 5.7 million to 7.7 million in less than eight years (from April 1962 to January 1970) was down to 6.4 million ten years later (in January 1980) clearly establishes the dramatic demographic impact of the 1970s. To more precisely estimate the number of excess deaths by 1970 age groups, each five-year cohort is projected forward from 1970 to 1980 and compared with its estimated size in 1980. The projection is based on normal mortality, simply extrapolated from the pre-1970 mortality trends, with about 200,000 emigrants to Vietnam between 1970 and 1975, and another 150,000 between 1975 and 1980. The residual of 2.41 million people, as shown in Table 5-1, can now be attributed to the number of excess deaths among people born in 1970. These numbers can then be averaged with similar numbers obtained by retroprojecting the 1980 population back to 1970 by cohorts (above age ten). The result is slightly higher in this case (2.63 million) and the average of the two provides our estimate of excess deaths as 2.52 million for the decade.[11] Each parameter can be varied from its minimum to its maximum plausible value, yielding a range of 1.17 million to 3.42 million excess deaths for the decade.

To obtain the number of excess deaths corresponding strictly to the DK years requires ancillary estimates. As mentioned in a section above, 300,000 might be a reasonable estimate of the mortality impact of the

---

[11] As noted earlier, in a population that is growing, the residual based on the backward projection to the earlier population underestimates the actual number during the period, while the forward projection to the later population overestimates it. The contrary is happening here because population actually decreased between 1970 and 1980.

1970-1975 civil war, while a similar number might also be reasonable for the impact of the famine, although the range of estimates for the latter is quite wide. Finally, the excess mortality of those born after 1970 (not included in Table 5-1) is quite difficult to estimate because of the uncertainty about fertility. Its meaning is perhaps not intuitive either, since excess deaths have been defined as the difference between the actual number of deaths and the number of deaths predicted under normal demographic conditions. Thus, if fertility was halved and child mortality doubled, the number of excess deaths among these birth cohorts might be zero. In my best judgment, a rough approximation of the number of excess deaths for the 1970-1979 births might also be 300,000.[12] Combining a central estimate of 2.5 million for the decade, and approximations of 300,000 each for the mortality impact of the civil war, the death toll of the 1979 famine, and mortality of the 1970-1978 cohorts yields an estimate of 2.2 million excess deaths for the four years of the DK.

A Decomposition by Cause

The decomposition between natural and violent mortality was reached by modeling natural mortality using the high-mortality pattern in Preston et al. (1993) life tables corresponding to life expectancies at birth for both males and females to 12 years.[13] The corresponding pattern is shown in

---

[12] Table 5-1 shows about 400,000 excess deaths in the youngest five-year age groups and Figure 5-1 shows that the excess mortality rate is going up for males and down for females at the youngest ages. We may thus assume that under the same fertility and mortality conditions, the number of excess deaths among the next cohorts would also be in the order of 400,000 for each five-year birth cohort. But the 1970-1975 birth cohorts might have been about 20 percent smaller because of reduced fertility in the period, and by 1975 their cohort size relative to earlier cohorts might have been reduced further because of the 1970-1975 mortality increase that affected the youngest ages most. Thus among the 1970-1975 birth cohorts, the total number of deaths between 1975 and 1979 was reduced by perhaps 25 percent or more, and excess deaths, as defined here, probably fell below 300,000 for those cohorts. A similar reasoning suggests that the number of excess deaths should not be very large among the 1975-1978 birth cohorts. First, the initial size of these cohorts might have been reduced by as much as 50 percent. Then, normal mortality is also higher among these cohorts than among earlier cohorts whose members were older in the period (because normal mortality declines from birth to late childhood).

[13] This estimate of life expectancy at birth accounts only for natural mortality causes (including famine) and refers to the 1975-1979 period only. An estimate of life expectancy including all causes of death can be derived by age-specific growth rates method (Preston and Bennett, 1983) for the 1972-1979 period, the shortest period for which reasonable estimates of starting and ending populations can be obtained by age and sex. The corresponding life expectancies at age five are 14.4 years for males and 22.0 years for females. Maximum estimates of life expectancy at birth during the DK period can be obtained for each sex by combining the 1972-1979 expectancy at age five with the 0-5 mortality corresponding to

Figure 5-4, together with the pattern of residual mortality. The decomposition yields plausible results, including a residual number of violent deaths of 1.1 million deaths for the 1975-1979 period. This estimate is one half of the total number of excess deaths during the DK estimated above, a proportion consistent with direct reports about causes of death (Heder, 1997; Sliwinski, 1995). The residual age pattern is also plausible overall. Male violent mortality exceeds female violent mortality in adulthood, especially for younger adults. The male age pattern clearly exhibits a peak for men in their teens in 1970 (seven years older, on average, during the DK). More surprising is the female violent mortality peak in older adulthood, matching male mortality. As the elite of the former government was initially the prime target of the Khmers Rouges, a mortality peak in those ages is plausible even though executions became less and less confined to that group. A second surprising finding is the violent mortality rate of children. It is possible that these high rates indeed reflect the residual mortality of the children of adult victims, especially their youngest children. A less sinister explanation would be the relative underestimation of the natural mortality of children (under age 15) compared to that of young adults. Our model age pattern of natural mortality is lowest for the 10- to 14-year olds, but as discussed above their mortality might actually be higher than that of young adults under famine conditions.[14]

In closing, I must apologize for spending so much more space on my own efforts to assess what happened in Cambodia during the 1970s. This bias reflects no belief that these efforts were more successful than others were. As argued elsewhere (Heuveline, 1998b), the uncertainty surrounding any single attempt is too large to attach much confidence to any single

---

a life expectancy at birth of 12 years in the Preston et al. (1993) life tables. The resulting estimates, 6.6 years for males and 10.9 years for females, likely overestimate life expectancy at birth during the DK. First, they do not account for violent mortality from birth to age five, and second, beyond age five they are based on averages for the 1972-1979 period while mortality was most intense between 1975 and 1978.

[14] Of course, the possibility of bad data always provides alternative explanations. Too many excess deaths would be produced by overestimating the size of the cohort in 1970 and underestimating its size in 1980. For the cohorts under age 10 in 1970, a large underestimation in 1980 is unlikely. The reasons are first that these people were aged 23 to 33 during the 1993 electoral registration, ages that are believed to have been comparatively well registered. Second, the normal mortality of young adults is low and thus the results of the backward projection from 1993 to 1980 show little sensitivity to the mortality assumptions made for the period. An overestimation of the size of these cohorts in 1970 might be produced by overestimating fertility and underestimating mortality between 1962 and 1970. In my estimation, the lowest plausible fertility and highest plausible mortality assumption would reduce the number of excess deaths among 1960-1970 birth cohorts by a third, still more than 500,000. For a fuller discussion of results elasticity to the different parameters of the demographic reconstruction, see Heuveline (1998a).

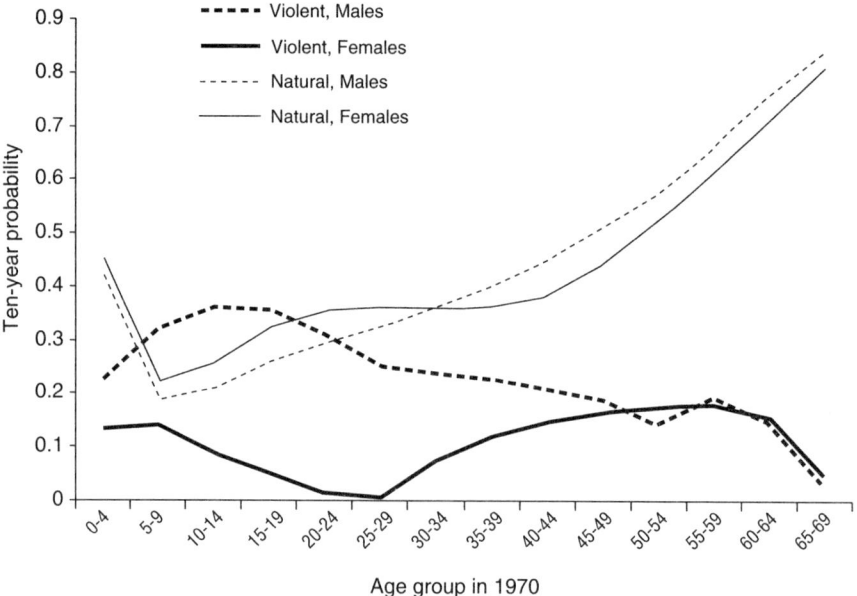

FIGURE 5-4 Sex-, age-, and cause-specific pattern of mortality in Cambodia, ten-year probability of dying, 1970-1979. Source: Adapted from Heuveline (1998a) and Preston et al. (1993).

estimate. In the end, it is rather from the limited convergence of some of these independent attempts that a sense of confidence might be gained. The disproportionate emphasis resulted from wanting to describe the different considerations and difficult decisions that the analyst must face to customize existing techniques to the available data and the expected pattern of mortality crisis, while being of course most familiar with those involved in my own work.

How can the available estimates and techniques be improved? New data can always be collected. The 1998 General Census of Cambodia will contribute to refine the estimation of the post-1980 trends. As the country becomes more accessible a small team of dedicated investigators may collect better survey data before survivors' memory begin to decline (see for instance, a related study in Vietnam by Hirschman et al., 1995). Per-haps mortality models that have proved so useful to estimate "normal" mortality in populations with poor data could also be developed for mor-tality crises. The example of Cambodia suggests that a general pattern would not be applicable to all situations, but models could probably be developed to fit a typology of such crises as one might emerge from this volume. Preston et al. (1993) already developed a model of high mortality that may apply to crises characterized primarily by a rise in infectious diseases,[15] as may affect refugees or urban populations when basic services have collapsed. As mentioned above, data on famine mortality appears to show a consistent pattern, close to the former one, except perhaps for young adults. A third distinct pattern is that of war casualties, which predominantly affects young adult males. This pattern will be more manifest the more those casualties are confined to combatants. In the case of Cambodia, military and political violence affected civilians as well through bombardments, landmines, and widespread executions. This fourth set of causes of death was probably less distinctly age patterned and made the characterization of the Cambodian mortality pattern of the 1970s even more difficult.

REFERENCES

Ashton, B., K. Hill, A. Piazza, and R. Zeitz
1984 Famine in China, 1958-61. *Population and Development Review* 10(4):613-645.
Banister, J.
1993 *Vietnam: Population Dynamics and Prospects, Indonesia Research Monograph 6.* Berkeley: Institute of East Asian Studies, University of California at Berkeley.
Banister, J., and E. Paige Johnson
1993 After the Nightmare: The Population of Cambodia. Pp. 65-140 in Benedict Kiernan, ed., *Genocide and Democracy in Cambodia: The Khmer Rouge, the United Nations and the International Community.* New Haven: Southeast Asia Studies, Yale University.
Barbieri, M., J. Allman, B.S. Pham, and M.T. Nguyen
1995 La situation demographique du Viet Nam. *Population* 50(3):621-652.
Bhat, M.P.N.
1987 *Mortality in India: Levels, Trends, and Patterns.* Unpublished Ph.D. Dissertation, University of Pennsylvania.
Brass, W.
1975 *Methods for Estimating Fertility and Mortality from Limited and Defective Data.* Chapel Hill, NC: Carolina Population Center, Laboratories for Population Studies.
Chandler, D.P.
1996 *A History of Cambodia.* 2nd ed., updated ed. Boulder, Colorado and Oxford, U.K.: Westview Press.
Chandra Sekar, C., and W.E. Deming
1949 On a method of estimating birth and death rates and the extent of registration. *Journal of the American Statistical Association* 44(1):101-115.
Coale, A.J., and P. Demeny
1983 *Regional Model Life Tables and Stable Populations.* 2nd ed. with Barbara Vaughan. New York: Academic Press.

---

[15] These models are based on the mortality experience of American immigrants to Liberia in the 19th century. The cause of death most responsible for their extremely high mortality was malaria infection.

Ea, M.T.
  1981   Kampuchea: A country adrift. *Population and Development Review* 7(2):209-228.
  1987   Recent Population Trends in Kampuchea. Pp. 3-15 in David A. Ablin and
         Marlowe Hood, eds., *The Cambodian Agony*. Armonk, New York: M. E. Sharpe.
Heder, S.
  1997   [Personal communication].
Heuveline, P.
  1998a "Between one and three million": Towards the demographic reconstruction of a
         decade of Cambodian history (1970-79). *Population Studies* 52(1):49-65.
  1998b L'insoutenable incertitude du nombre: Estimation des décès de la période Khmer
         Rouge. *Population* 53(6):1103-1118.
Hill, K.
  1987   New approaches to the estimation of migration flows from census and adminis-
         trative data sources. *International Migration Review* 21(4):1279-1303.
Hirschman, C., S. Preston, and M.L. Vu
  1995   Vietnamese casualties during the American War: A new estimate. *Population and
         Development Review* 21(4):783-812.
Huguet, J.
  1992   The demographic situation in Cambodia. *Asia-Pacific Population Journal* 6(4):79-
         91.
  1997   *The Population of Cambodia, 1980-1996, and Projected to 2000.* Phnom Penh, Cambo-
         dia: United Nations Population Fund for the National Institute of Statistics, Min-
         istry of Planning.
Kiernan, B.
  1986   Review essay: William Shawcross, declining Cambodia. *Bulletin of Concerned
         Asian Scholars* 18(1):56-63.
  1989   The American bombardment of Kampuchea, 1969-1973. *Vietnam Generation*
         1(1):4-42.
  1996   *The Pol Pot Regime.* New Haven and London: Yale University Press.
Lebrun, F.
  1971   Les hommes et la mort en Anjou aux XVIIe et XVIIIe siècle: Essai de démographie
         et de psychologie historiques. In *Civilisations et Societés 25.* Paris and La Haye:
         Mouton.
Lee, R.D.
  1997   Population Dynamics: Equilibrium, Disequilibrium, and Consequences of Fluc-
         tuations. In Mark R. Rosenzweig and Oded Stark, eds., *Handbook of Population
         and Family Economics*, vol. 1B. Amsterdam: Elsevier Science B.V.
Maharatna, A.
  1996   *The Demography of Famines: An Indian Historical Perspective.* Delhi: Oxford Univer-
         sity Press.
Martorell, R., and T.J. Ho
  1984   Malnutrition, Morbidity, and Mortality. In W. Henry Mosley, and Lincoln C.
         Chen, eds., *Child Survival: Strategies for Research. Population and Development Re-
         view* 10(Supp.):49-68.
Migozzi, J.
  1973   *Cambodge: Faits et problèmes de population.* Paris: Editions du Centre National de la
         Recherche Scientifique.
Murray, C.J.L., and L.C. Chen
  1994   Dynamics and patterns of mortality change. Pp. 3-23 in Lincoln C. Chen, Arthur
         Kleinman, and Norma C. Ware, eds., *Health and Social Change in International
         Perspective,* Harvard Series on Population and International Health. Cambridge,
         MA: Harvard University Press.

National Institute of Statistics

    1996   *Demographic Survey of Cambodia: General Report.* Phnom Penh, Cambodia: United Nations Population Fund for the National Institute of Statistics, Ministry of Planning.

    1999   *General Population Census of Cambodia 1998: Final Census Results.* Phnom Penh, Cambodia: United Nations Population Fund for the National Institute of Statistics, Ministry of Planning.

Preston, S.H.

    1976   Causes of Death and Age Patterns of Mortality. Pp. 89-119 in Samuel H. Preston, *Mortality Patterns in National Populations, With Special Reference to Recorded Causes of Death.* New York, San Francisco, London: Academic Press.

Preston, S.H., and N.G. Bennett

    1983   A census-based method for estimating adult mortality. *Population Studies* 37(1):91-104.

Preston, S.H., P. Heuveline, and M. Guillot

    2001   *Demography: Measuring and Modeling Population Processes.* Oxford, England: Blackwell Publishers.

Preston, S.H., and K. Hill

    1980   Estimating the completeness of registration data. *Population Studies* 34(2):349-366.

Preston, S.H., A. McDaniel, and C. Grushka

    1993   New model life tables for high-mortality populations. *Historical Methods* 26(4):149-159.

Rogers, A., and L.J. Castro

    1981   *Model Migration Schedules.* Laxenburg, Austria: International Institute for Applied Systems Analysis.

Shryock, H.S., and J.S. Siegel

    1975   *The Methods and Materials of Demography.* Washington, D.C.: U.S. Government Printing Office.

Siampos, G.S.

    1970   The population of Cambodia, 1945-1980. *Milbank Memorial Fund Quarterly* 48:317-360.

Sihanouk, N.

    1986   *Prisonnier des Khmers Rouges.* Paris: Hachette.

Sliwinski, M.

    1995   *Le génocide Khmer Rouge: Une analyse démographique.* Paris: L'Harmattan.

Ung, L.

    2000   *First They Killed My Father: A Daughter of Cambodia Remembers.* New York: HarperCollins.

United Nations

    1983   *Manual X: Indirect Techniques for Demographic Estimation.* New York: United Nations.

    1995   *United Nations in Cambodia.* New York: United Nations.

U.S. Bureau of the Census

    1991   *World Population Profile, 1991.* Washington, D.C.: U.S. Government Printing Office.

Vickery, M.

    1988   How many died in Pol Pot's Kampuchea? *Bulletin of Concerned Asian Scholars* 20(1):70-73.

6

Reflections

Manuel Carballo

So-called "excess" mortality is typically the most dramatic outcome of complex emergencies and natural disasters, and humanitarian and disaster relief operations have traditionally and rightly been tasked with reducing or averting it to the extent possible. As a result of the attention that has been given to this over the course of the last two decades, major inroads have been made with respect to understanding the dynamics of excess mortality in crisis situations and in identifying the interventions best suited to those situations. Thus, although averting excess mortality continues to be a constant challenge for relief workers, the knowledge that has been acquired is making the problem all the more amenable to intervention.

Over the years, mortality data have also become valuable indicators of the impact of focused health interventions such as emergency vaccination and feeding as well as the impact of more general operations such as organized evacuation. The donor and the relief community have thus seen fit to refer to mortality statistics in determining the "natural history" of emergencies and in identifying the type, scope, and duration of the assistance required. In much the same way, changing patterns of mortality have been increasingly used as descriptors of impending natural disasters such as famine, and man-made ones such as conflict and ethnic cleansing.

Using mortality data as indicators of past, existing, or forthcoming disasters, and by extension, of the need for relief interventions, nevertheless presents a number of conceptual and methodological challenges.

Some of these have become more evident as a result of recent crises in different parts of the world, and the papers in this volume are particularly valuable in drawing our attention to the issues involved.

Any discussion on the use of health statistics, for example, must consider the perennial question of denominator data and the difficulties that are almost inevitably encountered in obtaining these in the context of complex emergencies and natural disasters. Knowing what the risks are and who is really "at risk" are questions that have long plagued the assessment of complex emergencies and natural disasters and their health impact.

There are no easy solutions to this, especially where national health and other statistics prior to and certainly during crises have been poorly kept, tampered with, or damaged, or are simply not accessible. The papers discussed here reflect these difficulties and rightly raise them as limiting factors in any discussion of mortality in the context of emergencies and disasters. More attention clearly needs to be given to accessing denominator data from countries where the perceived likelihood of complex emergencies and natural disasters is high. It is also important that more attention is given to defining the risk factors and events that are likely to be of concern in crisis situations so that planning for data needs can occur early on. Burkholder et al., for example, refers to "war-related deaths" and highlights the question of what are war-related deaths. Are they the deaths that result from war injuries? Are deaths associated with "unintentional" injuries and exposure that occur during flight from persecution and accidents *en route* to safe havens to be included? And what about deaths that occur as a result of lack of access to health care services and medication? Shall we include the deaths among the elderly and others who "give up" the will to live in these situations? And what of the suicides that so often occur but also go unmeasured? If the latter are to be included, and surely the case must be made for this, then the concept of war-related deaths takes on a whole new scope and importance.

In the same way, it is important that we try to distinguish between mortality in the location of the crisis (e.g., primarily intentional and unintentional injuries and homicide), mortality during uprooting and forced movement (e.g., primarily "natural" causes, unintentional and intentional injuries), and mortality during resettlement (e.g., primarily "natural" causes and unintentional injuries).

Robinson et al.'s data suggest that in the case of North Korea the movement of people was not associated with mortality either as a prompting event or as an associated impact. In the case of Kosovo, on the other hand, at least two and possibly three very different pictures emerged. Mortality, or the fear of it, was a major prompting event, as it often is in situations of ethnic cleansing. There is also evidence that mortality peaked around the time the international community took retaliatory measures, and here a confusing image of intentional and unintentional injuries, homicide and genocide will no doubt prove difficult to unravel for a variety of reasons, some of which are discussed below.

The International Centre for Migration and Health (ICMH) also found considerable anecdotal information to the effect that deaths *en route* to Albania and Macedonia were relatively high among the elderly and newborn infants in the context of complicated pregnancies and deliveries in hostile physical environments where there was little qualified care. By contrast, mortality in refugee camps in Albania and Macedonia was relatively low, pointing not only to the adequacy of the relief operations by national receiving governments and external organizations, but also to the fact that most refugees were probably relatively healthy at the time the exodus began.

Here we are reminded of how each emergency or natural disaster deserves to be approached as a unique event. For while there may be many shared characteristics and processes, it is in the uniqueness of each event that the challenge of planning and implementing relief lies. Unfortunately, some of the relief organizations responding to the Kosovo crisis built operations on experiences gained in other parts of the world where mortality related to malnutrition, infectious diseases, waterborne infections, and unhealthy environmental conditions has traditionally been the problem. In the case of refugees in Albania and Macedonia, however, the problem quickly became more one of chronic diseases whose management called for a different category of support and medical supplies, a fact which, just as during the war in Bosnia, often caught relief organizations unprepared.

There is also a need to highlight the importance of disaggregating mortality, or indeed any health-related data, by at least age, sex, and family status. Not to do so puts into question the usefulness of mortality (and other health) data from the perspective of understanding both the epidemiology of mortality itself and its implications for surviving populations. For especially (but not only) in emergency and disaster situations the death of any individual has the potential to implicate and threaten the health and well being of others in many and profound ways. The precocious rupture of symbiotic relationships between people, particularly within families, can have an immediate impact on the welfare of survivors, be they children, women, the elderly, or indeed men. It is noteworthy, for example, that Robinson et al. found that widows were more vulnerable. And when Burkholder et al. refer to the high mortality rate among the elderly, this was probably due not only to natural attrition in the harsh conditions of forced uprooting and movement, but also to the fact that many were "unaccompanied" and possibly without the help of relatives and close family.

From a more methodological perspective the papers also highlight the realities and shortcomings encountered in enumerating anything, including health events in complex emergencies and natural disasters. For even when events are readily discernible and measurable in principle, the fact remains that from a logistical perspective they often occur in situations from which it is difficult (and at times dangerous) to gather reliable information. The papers also remind us of the fact that while mortality data may be important to relief organizations from the point of view of knowing when, how, and with what to intervene from an international perspective, they are sometimes not seen in the same light from a national point of view.

There are a number of reasons why national partners may view these data differently. In countries where ethnic hostilities and political strife are the cause of excess mortality, information can be politically sensitive and, at best, susceptible to under- or over-reporting. Because they can be indicative of things that are going wrong, mortality data are often defended by countries and interested parties as highly private and confidential. When they are, they also tend to be hidden, tampered with, or purposely skewed. In this regard, Robinson et al. highlight the importance of using creative techniques for generating mortality data while at the same time reminding us of the difficulties involved in developing sensitive and specific methods for doing so. The papers in this volume are an important reminder of how easily mortality data (and mortality itself) can be hidden unless innovative and creative techniques are used to extract and put together relevant images of excess mortality.

Burkholder et al. refer to the difficulties that many external relief groups had in accessing data that had been gathered by national health services in Albania and Macedonia. While this limited access can be criticized, the other reality is that the relationship between external groups and national governments receiving refugees is often so ill defined that governments are not clear as to why health data (or other information) are being requested and how they will be used. In Albania and Macedonia, the lack of a good working relationship between relief organizations and national and local government was already evident in the first week of April 1999. It did not improve significantly for a variety of reasons, some of which were probably preventable. In the case of Macedonia, where large numbers of refugees had been accommodated from the very beginning of the crisis in local communities, the government felt that it was being unduly recognized for what it had done to assist. External groups were arriving and setting up relief operations, often bypassing national and local governments. The authorities were also concerned about the impact refugees would have on local health services and the capacity of those services to respond to both refugees and national populations.

ICMH studies of this phenomenon in other parts of the world have pointed to the relatively cavalier way in which local health systems and authorities are often neglected by relief organizations in both planning and implementing relief operations. Yet no matter how comprehensive relief interventions are, referral of complicated cases always depends on the capacity of local health services to accommodate them. The additional "load" this represents is rarely reflected in the support they get from relief organizations.

In the case of Albania, where the health care system has been under-funded and over-stretched for the past five or so years, local authorities were concerned about their capacity to respond appropriately (although, just as in Macedonia, they did respond well). They were also critical of how little they were invited to participate in some of the relief planning operations that would ultimately have an impact on local services as well. Making access to health-related data difficult to external groups under such circumstances may often be a reaction to how they feel they are being treated.

In the context of the Kosovo crisis, poor coordination and communication between different relief agencies also stood out as a major problem that while not unique to that situation, nevertheless had serious implications for data generation and planning in general. The proliferation of relief agencies and groups often became a challenge as well as a contribution. Some came with different mandates, interests, and degrees of experience and technical sophistication. Their interest in and capacity for gathering health-related data in general and mortality data in particular varied considerably. More importantly, their commitment to sharing data (or even understanding why health data should be pooled) also varied and different methods of data collection were often used and the possibilities of using standardized techniques were typically neglected.

The fact that health-related data are useful in generating support from donors and in reporting back to them on the impact of relief operations also, no doubt, tended to make pooling of information even more of a challenge. Traditionally this has often thrown into question the reliability of data generated by relief groups because of fears that it would be imprecise and either over- or underestimated.

The lack of coordination and pooling of health data also had its implications for the interventions formulated by different groups, and there is no doubt that duplication, contradictions in approaches, over-focusing on some issues and neglecting others occurred as a result. Coordination, or the lack of it, thus stood out as one of the most difficult issues in general, and especially so in the collection of mortality and other health statistics.

Finally, although mortality statistics are of paramount importance in understanding the severity of crisis situations, we must not lose sight of the fact that they provide only a restricted image of those crises. However, because they do reflect such a visible part of the problem, there is a danger that at times the collection of mortality statistics and activities designed to reduce excess mortality will eclipse other equally salient but less evident concerns. Thus, for example, the issue of psychosocial morbidity, and I would even dare to say, mortality, has been neglected as an issue even though from the point of view of long-term disability and limitations to social reconstruction and recovery, this may be of equally significant importance as physical mortality.

Index

A

Accidental injuries, 131, 132
    Cambodians, 113
    Kosovars, 92
    North Koreans, 74
Afghanistan, 38-41
Africa, 6
    ECOMOG, 47
    see also Angola; Burundi; Eritrea;
        Ethiopia; Liberia; Mozambique;
        Rwanda; Sierra Leone; Somalia;
        Sudan; Uganda; Zaire
Age factors, 2, 12, 14-20, 30, 34, 132
    Afghans, 40
    Bosnia, 14
    Cambodians, 17, 18, 19, 20, 102, 109-111,
        112-115, 116-117, 118, 121-126, 127
    camp populations, general, 14, 15-17
    crude mortality rates, 30, 39, 63
    gender factors and, 16, 17-20, 30, 45, 62,
        63, 114, 121-123, 124-126, 127, 132
    Kosovars, 89, 95-97, 99
    North Koreans, 18, 73, 74, 79, 84
    Rwandans, 15-16, 55, 61, 62, 63
    see also Children; Elderly persons;
        Life expectancy
Aid, *see* Humanitarian interventions
Albania, Kosovars in, *see* Kosovo

Alliance des Forces Démocratiques de
    Libération du Congo-Zaire
    (AFDL), 53, 57, 59
Angola, 5, 10, 25
Asia, *see* Afghanistan; Cambodia; China;
    Iran; Iraq; North Korea; Pakistan;
    Soviet Union, dissolution of;
    Thailand; Vietnam

B

Balkans, 22, 25
    see also Bosnia; Kosovo; Macedonia
Bangladesh, 5, 9, 13
Baseline mortality
    defined, 4
    Kosovars, 90, 99
Birth rate, *see* Fertility
Bosnia, 10, 24, 25, 26, 39, 41-43
    age factors, 14
    crude mortality rates, 41
    executions, 41
    forensics, 41-42
    gender factors, 41
    mass graves, 41-42
    medical interventions, 42-43
    urban areas, 41, 42-43
Burundi, 53